Bob Urichuck

Up your bottom line

Featuring the ABC, 123 Sales Results System

*Lifestyle resources for personal growth
and enhanced performance*

Published by Creative Bound Inc.
P.O. Box 424, Carp, Ontario
Canada K0A 1L0
(613) 831-3641
www.creativebound.com

ISBN 0-921165-72-2
Printed and bound in Canada

© 2001 Bob Urichuck

Editing: Janet Shorten
Book design: Wendelina O'Keefe
Author photograph: Teckles Photography

printing number 10 9 8 7 6 5 4 3 2 1

Canadian Cataloguing in Publication Data

Urichuck, Robert
    Up your bottom line : featuring the ABC, 123 sales results
system

ISBN 0-921165-72-2

1. Selling. I. Title.

HF5439.5.U75 2001   658.8'1   C2001-900253-X

To my parents, who gave me the opportunity to realize that the world revolves around sales.

To my loving wife, Joan, and my wonderful sons, Michael and David, who have supported and encouraged me in all endeavors.

Bob,

Thanks for meeting with me.

May 9, 2002

A-3-K- more to sell more!

Bobby.

Preface

The ABC, 123 Sales Results System represents many years of personal selling experience—experience gained through acceptance and rejection, good times and bad times, success and failure.

Sales has been a way of life for me since I was a boy. I was raised in a small family business and, thanks to both of my parents, I was exposed to the world of sales. You might say I was raised to be in sales, and for that I am really grateful.

By the time I was a teenager, all of my brothers and sisters knew how to bake bread. I didn't, but I knew how to sell, and make a different form of bread—money. I learned at a young age that without a sale, there is no money. If there was no money, my parents couldn't make any bread, and we couldn't eat. I realized the world revolved around sales.

As I grew older I found that sales was not always a respected profession, but I studied business in college anyway. It was unbelievable. I was an A student and I graduated with honors. Why? Because of the sales and business experience I had gained as a child. Again, thanks to both of my parents.

It wasn't long after graduating that I realized that the profession of sales was for me. I got involved in multi-level and network marketing, became a door-to-door salesperson and later joined a major oil corporation in a sales and marketing capacity. I had a passion for land development and started developing and selling land. I then got involved with the majors—Canada's leading land developers and builders—in mass sales and large-price boardroom selling. Up until this point I had no formal sales training.

Then later in life, while working with a major Canadian corporation, I positioned myself into sales training. I was able to witness over 30 major

North American sales training programs in one year. While I was doing my job and recommending a program to the organization, I also did a best-practice analysis and created my own system, the ABC, 123 Sales Results System.

This book is dedicated to those who have decided to improve their selling skills in order to increase their sales effectiveness and improve the quality of their lives and the lives of others with whom they come in contact.

Contents

Introduction

Markets around the world are heating up. Competitors are appearing out of nowhere and expectations are high, especially from top management. In today's market, corporate business executives, business owners and seasoned professional salespeople have to be producing at their absolute best to stay up with the industry leaders.

A business person is a sales professional who today has to be proactive, highly energetic, entrepreneurial, self-driven, efficient and aware of the bottom line. He or she needs to be honest, sensitive, a master problem solver and above all, a personal marketing genius with a win/win philosophy.

With this in mind, I designed a sales results system to help business people develop all the above characteristics and skills, and more. The profession of being a salesperson is no different than any other profession. All professionals go through years of training and continuous learning. The main difference in the sales profession, though, and one that you must learn to deal with, is the amount of rejection that you can face in one day.

Traditional training has taught us many techniques to handle objections, but none for rejection. Over the years we have taught buyers these techniques, because all salespeople were using them. In turn, buyers have created their own system to deal with salespeople; they now qualify us and have control over the selling process. In order for salespeople to be successful, they must maintain control over the sales process. To do that, they must be different from the last salesperson that visited the buyer. In order to succeed sales professionals must have a step-by-step sales results system to follow.

The sales results system that I developed after years of research and application is based on non-traditional techniques that give you the edge.

It is a proven system, known internationally as the ABC, 123 Sales Results System.

Attitude

You can't build anything without a solid foundation. The **"A"** is for **Attitude**—the foundation of all successful people. Attitude is the "advance person" of our true selves. Its roots are inward, based on past experiences, but its fruit is outward. It is our best friend, or our worst enemy. It is more honest and more consistent than our words. It is the thing that either draws people to us or repels them. It is never content until it is expressed. It is the librarian of our past, the speaker of our present, and the prophet of our future. Yet who is in control of your attitude?

1. **You** are 100 percent in control of your attitude! There are a lot of things in life we have no control over. For example, there is absolutely nothing we can do about how prospects react to us or our products and services. All we can do is control the way we react. Yet so many salespeople let the prospect's reaction determine their outlook for the day. Think about it: are you as positive, upbeat and driven on a day full of rejection as you are on a highly successful day?

    How do you react to negative prospects? Do you walk away discouraged and complain about it or do you take control, stay focused and go on to the next call? Success is based on good judgment and good judgment is based on experience and the only way one can gain experience is through failure. Isn't sales a numbers game? We have to fail often to succeed once.

    This is all about attitude. How you react, how you think, what you say to yourself and what you believe about yourself are all under your control and are reflected in your attitude. You must first realize that your attitude is 100 percent under your control and then learn to reflect, confirm and take hold of your attitude. You must take hold of your attitude toward yourself, overcome fear and learn to deal with rejection in order to increase your productivity while saving time and money.

2. What is your attitude toward your **organization**, its team players and products and services? Do you have an owner's mentality? If so, what would you do differently? Now, why are you not doing it? You have to address these issues and have a strong belief before you can move on.

3. What is your attitude toward the **market** that you represent? Do you have a clear full-color picture of your ideal prospect? Do you know your competition and their strengths and weaknesses? If you don't, is it fair to say that you don't know what you are doing?

If you don't believe in (1) yourself, (2) the organization that you represent, its team, products and services and (3) the market that you are selling in, move on and find something you do believe in. How could you convince anyone else to believe in something that you yourself don't believe in?

Behavior

You can have a fantastic attitude, but a positive attitude alone is not enough to guarantee long-term success. You need goals and an action plan to get where you want to go. The **"B"** stands for **Behavior**. Behavior is the manner in which you conduct yourself. It is the way you behave, the way you act, function or react. The 1,2,3's are the goals and behaviors from a personal, organizational and market targeting level. Without goals there is no reason to act, no motivation to take daily actions or go the extra mile.

1. Appropriate behavior drives opportunities. Opportunities come from setting goals, written S.M.A.R.T. goals. What do you want out of life or out of your business? Who can determine this for you and who can make it happen? What are the daily behaviors that you must apply to live the life of **your dreams**?

2. It is those daily behaviors, when you implement them, that will make a big difference in your level of sales success in **your organization**. For example, as salespeople we need to constantly network, call on prospects, qualify them, present, help them buy and follow up with

them. When is the best time to be conducting these behaviors? Naturally, it is when the prospect or client is available. So let's refer to these behaviors as "pay-time" behaviors—those behaviors that lead us to the accomplishment of our goals or sales quotas. What are the pay-time behaviors that you need to conduct on a daily basis to meet your goals and when do you need to conduct them?

We all know that sales is more than being in front of customers. Like any other profession we need time for internal communications, training, paperwork and other forms of administration. These are activities or behaviors that are necessary but do not directly provide us with revenue. Let's refer to these behaviors as "no-pay-time" behaviors.

When we look at our week and each day, we must plan and determine time slots for both types of behaviors, pay time and no-pay time. What are the best times of the day for you to be in front of customers or to be contacting them? What are the worst times? It is during these worst times that you should be conducting no-pay-time behaviors. Once you identify these behaviors and times and stick to them, watch your time management skills and results improve dramatically.

3. What about **your market**? Does 80% of your business come from 20% of your customers? If so, what does your 20% look like? Can you clearly define them? Now, where should you be spending your time? I have found that it takes more time to sell smaller accounts that produce less revenue than selling large accounts that produce more revenue. If you take the time to define your absolute, beneficial and convenient. (A,B,C) criteria you will have a better handle on who you should be targeting in on—that is, if you want a maximum return on your investment in time. Then as you target in, you will be in a better position to obtain pertinent industry, organizational and client information.

Competencies

Now, with a fantastic attitude and appropriate goal-driven behaviors, you sneed to add the "**C**," which stands for **Competencies**. You need the competencies of your profession, as lawyers or doctors need them for theirs. Where can you develop your competencies? As salespeople we can develop our competencies from reading books, in-class training, on the job, being coached or through trial and error. We can join professional sales associations, and in some countries we can even get certified as a sales professional.

The competencies that salespeople need are numerous but boil down to human interaction, communication and relationship building. Gone are the traditional days of the slick, hit-and-run "feature and benefit" dumps. Why? Because every buyer has been educated by us in the past and they have created their own system to maintain control over us. Now, it is a clear-cut case of being professional and following a non-traditional proven sales results system—that is, if we want to be different from everyone else out there. A system that will help you to establish rapport and build trust, to communicate effectively and to develop and maintain lasting relationships. A system that will put you in control and enable you to quickly qualify prospects on several levels, to determine next steps, to prescribe solutions, to let the prospect or customer buy, and to retain and develop client relationships leading to more business.

Without a sales results system, salespeople are working on a hit and miss basis, wasting time and not getting the results they could be getting. They become a slave to the buyer's system. A professionally trained salesperson following a sales results system is a very powerful tool in any organization. Remember, without sales, organizations don't exist. Let me share my system with you.

1. In order to build a long-term **relationship**, one must first establish rapport. You need to know the components of the rapport pie and how to build rapport in the first 30 seconds of meeting. You must know how to identify an individual's predominant sense and how to use that sense to your benefit during the presentation phase.

    Once rapport has been established, questions can be asked. However, you need to know why questions are so important, the types of questions that should be asked, and how to deal with questions from the prospect or client without giving free consulting. There are several series of questioning techniques that are available to salespeople. Let me share a few with you.

First, what problems, or pleasures, do you provide a solution to? List them. Now, develop a series of questions to uncover the problems. Use open-ended questions to get the prospect talking. As they speak, listen for clues. Question their answers. Seek clarification. Ask them directing questions leading to where you want to take them. Then start gathering facts and use closed-ended questions. It is like taking them through a self-discovery funnel. What do you think happens as they pop out of the spout of the funnel? And who was in control of the process?

When asking questions, you must listen effectively. Do you know what you should be listening for? There are several active listening techniques that you should apply, but the main question is, do you really want to service the prospect or are you there for your own reasons? My favorite quote relating to sales is Cavett Robert's "Nobody cares how much you know, until they know how much you care." Only good questioning and listening techniques will help you help the prospect buy. How well do you know your own listening skills? Can you identify the characteristics of good and poor listeners? If so, great! Are you practicing them?

2. Now we can take the above techniques and use them to **qualify** opportunities by setting the parameters. This is setting the ground rules, eliminating surprises and having a clear future that both parties can work toward. It means being 100 percent honest and up front — finding out the prospect's time, objectives and agenda, and dealing with your biggest objections early on. It is not about you; it is about them! Without them we have nothing.

We ask questions to uncover the prospect's buying motivators. We are talking about uncovering buying motivators here, not just the organizational needs. This means the personal emotions of the prospect — the real reason why people buy. If there is no pain, there is no gain. If there is no desire, there is no motivation. Your job is to find the pains or the desires, and not just one, but a few. This requires a trusting relationship combined with appropriate questioning techniques and excellent listening skills.

Once a number of buying motivators have been identified, you need to uncover financial considerations. This is a critical step in financially qualifying the prospect while providing you with information that will help you to suggest feasible solutions. If they don't have a budget, how will they proceed? If they do have a budget, you need to know what it is. How can you provide them with a solution if you don't know how much money they have set aside to satisfy their problems or desires?

Now that you have identified the buying motivators and the financial ability, you must confirm the decision-making process. When will the decision be made? Who besides the person you are speaking with is involved in the decision-making process? What will you do if a committee is involved? What if you cannot present to that committee? You must know how to deal with these situations in advance.

Once all the information in this step has been gathered, you need to summarize the findings by engaging the prospect or client in a committed way. Before you make this summary, buying motivators, financial ability, decision-making process and timing should all have been identified and qualified. This is where you determine if you have a solution to solve the prospect's problems or desires, within their budget, and if you can present it to the decision makers, or not. If not, abort. Why would you want to waste your time doing a presentation? Don't get trapped into the buyer's system.

However, if you have a solution to the prospect's problems or desires, within their budget, and they are ready to buy, and you can present to the decision maker(s), with a commitment of a yes or no answer after the presentation, the chances are you have the sale. Don't think any more; just do it. They are qualified. You are the doctor and you can prescribe a solution to their pain or pleasure—the two reasons that people buy.

3. You then need to **prescribe** solutions specific to the customer's needs, letting the customer buy, retaining the account, keeping competitors out and developing the account to its maximum potential. It sounds like a lot, but here is what you need to do.

First, review the parameters of the presentation, review the findings (pains or pleasures identified) and present prescribed solutions to the prospect's problems or desires, in their dominant sense. Then measure the prospect's reactions on prescriptions (solutions) identified for each problem. You can measure them by asking them how the solutions you have presented solve their problems or desires on a scale of words like "not" to "definitely" or from 1 to 10.

When you feel you have the prospect agreeing with your solutions, please don't go for a trial close. Don't push them. Just ask them what they would like you to do next. Learn to shut up. Let the prospect buy. Would you not prefer to buy rather than be sold?

Now you have a prospect that has purchased your prescription or solution. You now need to educate them on the other features and benefits of your product or service that you did not cover in your prescription, because you were only addressing problems or desires identified. Then you need to maintain the relationship, develop the account for more business and obtain new prospect introductions and referrals. That is simple. Do your job well and it will come. If not, ask and you shall receive.

Section A

• • •

The Bull's Eye Attitude:
Selling from the Inside Out

The Bull's Eye Attitude: Selling from the Inside Out

In this section we are going to discuss attitude—your attitude toward yourself, the organization you represent and the market you are selling in. But before we go forward on this journey we must understand what success, attitude and selling from the inside out mean.

Success means different things to different people. But let's look at salespeople. To a salesperson, success could be a major client acquisition, qualifying for an incentive, making a predetermined annual income or commission, being recognized at the annual sales conference as salesperson or team player of the year or simply meeting quota and maintaining a job. Each of us has different desires. The key is to determine your desires in sales and make it a goal to accomplish them. Success, you see, is the realization of a worthy goal or desire.

So what makes a successful salesperson? Obviously it is reaching their goals, but let's take a close look at the characteristics of successful salespeople. What would you identify as the top 10 characteristics of successful salespeople?

Over the years I have witnessed all kinds of responses. If I told you what the most popular 10 were, would it make a difference to what you wrote? You would think you were right or wrong. But what you wrote is right. What you didn't write is wrong. Take the time and write out 10 characteristics of successful salespeople based on what you have witnessed or desired for yourself.

Review your list. How many of these characteristics do you possess? How many of them do you want to possess? What must you do?

My intention is to help you to discover things for yourself. That is the only way that the learning will make a difference. Some of the characteristics that I hear regularly are the following: goal-driven, focused, communicates well—asks a lot of questions and listens well, organized, follows through, persistent, patient, honest, trustworthy, professional at all times, presents well, dresses well, cares, able to solve problems, results-oriented, doesn't take rejection personally, is enthusiastic and passionate about their profession, product or service and the organization they represent.

Identify the characteristics that you already have and the ones that you need to work on. Each month add one of those characteristics that you need to work on to your Monthly Monitor Chart (identified in Section B) and keep it identified on the chart until you have mastered that characteristic.

Now that we have identified some characteristics of successful salespeople, let's take a look from the other side of a sale—from the customer's point of view. Think of the last time you purchased something from a salesperson. How were you treated? As a customer, how would you like to be treated?

Like most customers, you probably want to be treated fairly and honestly. You want to be acknowledged, listened to, understood, appreciated and valued, shown respect, made to feel important, made to feel comfortable. But, as you know, this does not always happen when dealing with salespeople. How should you, as a professional salesperson, behave?

Let's take a look at the list above again. Is the way you are treated based on the attitude, behavior or competency of a salesperson?

You can say all three are the basis for being treated in a certain way. But where does it all start? With attitude. Attitude is the key success factor and the foundation of your success.

What is attitude? Attitude is your way of thinking or behaving. Your attitude toward people influences your behavior toward them. Your attitude affects your level of satisfaction with life, and with your job. Your attitude affects everyone who comes into contact with you. Your attitude is reflected in your tone of voice, posture and facial expressions. Your attitude can affect your health. It is your attitude that will make the biggest difference in your life—particularly when it comes to sales. Your past and present are a result of your past attitude. However, your present attitude will determine your future. The greatest thing about attitude is that it is not fixed and it is 100 percent under your control. Your attitude is up to you!

Whether you think you can, or you think you can't, you're absolutely right.

Henry Ford

Your attitude is created by your beliefs. Your beliefs were developed in your past. It may be time to re-evaluate them. Dig deep and make the necessary changes. Your present-day beliefs determine your attitude. It is your attitude that determines how you feel. How you feel determines how you act, and how you act determines your results in the realization of your dream.

Results
Actions
Feelings
Attitudes
Beliefs

Your self-image, your self-worth, your self-esteem and your self-confidence are all part of your attitude. How others see you, or perceive you, can influence your attitude, as it may have done in the past. That is external influence. If you accept that influence, whether it be positive or negative, you will let it affect you internally. However, if you become aware of those external influences and decide to lead from within, you can refuse to let them affect you. In this way, you start to take control of your attitude, and your life.

It all starts within *you*, the most important person in the world. You have to sell yourself on you, before you can sell anything to anybody.

A1 • YOU—The Bull's Eye Attitude

You are the most important person in the world and you are at the center of the bull's eye. Your attitude toward yourself is the bull's eye, the core of the target. Focus on the core of the target and you will hit the bull's eye more often. But to do that you need to know yourself.

One of the best ways to get to know yourself is to read and do the exercises in my first book, *Online for Life: The 12 Disciplines for Living Your Dreams* (see Bibliography). The discipline identified as #1 in *Online for Life* is **to know your rights**. There are 10 rights included under Discipline #1 in *Online for Life*, but I want to reinforce four rights here that are particularly important for salespeople.

1. You have the right to like yourself as you are.

> *Nothing splendid has ever been achieved except by those who dared believe that something inside of them was superior to circumstances.*
>
> Bruce Barton

Most of us go through life accepting too many external comments that lead us to believe that we are not good enough, attractive enough, strong enough, experienced enough . . . and the list goes on. Until we realize who we really are, we can fall into these traps and stay there.

In our younger years we picked up a lot of baggage. Some of it was good and some of it was not so good. Most of the time, as children, we believed what we were told. Many people received positive reinforcement, while others received negative comments. Anyone who was overweight, underweight, tall or short, handicapped or different, knows what I am talking about. The comments that we accepted as truth became part of us and led to our liking ourselves, or disliking ourselves, as we are.

We also compared ourselves to others and wished we had the looks, size, shape or qualities of someone else. Many times in our lives we may not have liked ourselves as we were, mostly because of external influences or comments. At other times, in certain environments, we liked ourselves as we were because of either internal beliefs or external influences and comments.

For example, as a young boy, my mother, aunts and grandmother would always grab my cheek and tell me how cute and how special I was because I had dimples. When I started going to school the girls told me I was cute. By the time I was 10, I believed I was cute.

By the time I became a teenager, life took a turn on me. Those cute dimples turned into ugly pimples. What do you think society told me then? Right, I was ugly. And the more times I would look into the mirror, the more I agreed with them. I was ugly. I became extremely shy. I avoided people, and avoided going out, basically losing five years of my life in the process.

Finally, someone approached me and told me about a girl who wanted to go to the graduation dance with me. It took me three weeks and a lot of courage to ask her. Shortly afterward, my wife-to-be looked beyond what she saw on the outside because the acne didn't matter to her. She gave me the gift of inner strength.

It was that new-found inner strength that caused me to wake up one day and look in the mirror again. As I looked in the mirror, I came to a great realization. Everyone has an outer shelter—skin—that they can hide behind. But it is what is behind that skin that really matters. Yes, I had acne, but I came to the conclusion that I liked the guy inside. As I realized this, I started to emerge from my shell. From that point on I decided to take control of my life and lead my life from the inside out, as opposed to the outside in. In fact, it was this inside-out approach that gave me the courage to eventually become a professional speaker and sales trainer.

Since then, I've liked myself as I am. I know myself, my values, my strengths and weaknesses, my dreams and desires.

Now let's take a look at this same process as it affects the role of a salesperson. Society could have influenced you to believe that the worst job in the world is to be a salesperson. Think about this for a moment. You are part of the general public and not a salesperson. Tell me what comes to mind when you hear the word "salesperson."

This is a valuable exercise in our training sessions. You see, most of us are raised to believe that we should become a professional of sorts. Sales was never considered as a serious profession until recently. When asked this question, even professional salespeople, acting as members of the general public, will use such words as "sleazy," "cheat," "money-hungry," "Herb Tarlic," "used-car salesman," "plaid suits," "sneaky," "liars," and so on, to describe salespeople.

Is that the image you want to portray? No. So what do you do? You hide behind other fancy titles like "account manager," "business development manager" or "product specialist." Why? Because you don't like being referred to as a salesperson. Yet are you any different? No. You keep doing what all other salespeople have done and eventually you will be perceived just as they are. Later, in Section C, I will show you how doing the opposite of traditional sales techniques will make you different and gain you a great deal of respect. So much respect that you will be proud to call yourself a salesperson.

As a certified sales professional I am very proud of my profession. Are you? If you are, you would have no problem, when you are putting your children to bed, telling them why they should grow up like you and be professional salespeople. Very few of us can do that, because of the general public perception of salespeople. How can you put your child to bed saying, I want you to grow to be a sleazy, money-hungry, used-car salesperson? Instead, we raise them to be doctors, lawyers and engineers. These professions are no different from ours. Each of them, like sales, requires the attitude, behavior and competencies of that profession. The main difference between these professions and the sales profession is the amount of respect salespeople have for their clients' time. Rarely does a sales professional have their client wait for them.

If you don't like yourself as a salesperson, or as you are, consider doing or being something different. As a salesperson, you have to have a passion for sales, a desire to solve other people's problems. But how can you solve their problems when you can't solve your own problems? You have to like yourself as you are, to believe in yourself, before anyone else will.

2. You have the right to fail.

Failure is the opportunity to begin again more intelligently.

Henry Ford

When society realizes the good that comes out of failure, and recognizes people for trying, the world will be better for it. All success comes from failure. No one in the world has succeeded without first trying, failing, learning, making changes, and moving on. Always remember that you have the right to fail; you no longer have to make excuses for your failed attempts. Instead, reflect on that failure and learn from it. That experience will provide you with better judgment for the future, and will eventually lead you to success.

Success is based on good judgment. Good judgment comes from experience. And how does one get experience? Sometimes we have to fail often to succeed once. But the fear of failure stops us from even trying. That is one of the reasons we procrastinate. We think about it too much; we hesitate. If you just do it and fail, what is the worst thing that can happen? You will learn a lesson. If you really want to succeed, you may have to double your failure rate. Isn't this what sales is all about?

After losing five years of my life hiding as a teenager with acne, I realized I had some catching up to do. I developed a "do it now" attitude. I no longer thought endlessly about things because I realized that the longer I thought about doing something, the longer I would hesitate before doing it; or I might not do it at all. I put procrastination behind me and started to just do things without thinking, realizing that the worst that can happen is that I will learn something.

Failure is part of my daily life. I don't always take the time to think things out. I am a doer. I learn and move forward by doing. This gives me lots of opportunities to fail, and to be criticized. I have experienced so much failure in my life that I am now wise because of it. I learn from every experience. I really see failure as a learning opportunity.

Are you giving yourself sufficient learning opportunities?

I believe that both failure and success are part of life's balance. The more you try, the more you fail, and the more you succeed. If you don't try, you'll neither fail nor succeed.

If you fear failure, you will almost certainly fail. Because of fear, many of us don't take action. We procrastinate. Fear paralyzes the faculty of reason, destroys the faculty of imagination, kills self-reliance, undermines enthusiasm, discourages initiative, leads to uncertainty of purpose, encourages procrastination, and makes self-control difficult. Fear removes the charm from a personality, destroys ambition, clouds memory and invites failure. It leads to sleeplessness, misery and unhappiness.

Fear is nothing more than a state of mind, and everyone has the ability to control his or her own state of mind. Do you think your fears are the same as everyone else's? Do you think they are justified by the real world? Are your fears my fears? Your fears are your fears and no one else's! Your fears exist only in your mind. Only you can overcome those fears.

The three biggest obstacles in life are indecision, doubt and fear. Indecision is the seed of fear. Indecision grows into doubt, and together the two become fear. We fear so many things, from failure to death. Some fears are justified. But other unnecessary fears can take root and grow unless you get rid of the seeds of indecision and doubt that grow into fear.

But before you can master fear, you must know its name, habits and where it comes from. When I was in my early twenties I was afraid to try public speaking. I was concerned that my language and my appearance were not good enough to stand in front of a crowd and speak. I dreaded rejection and criticism as a result of being criticized as a teenager by my friends. This fear prevented me from doing something I really wanted to do—to earn more by speaking to large groups.

Then, with some coaching, I developed enough self-confidence to finally give it a try. And the audience applauded! My fear could have set me back forever. Instead, I got on stage again the next day and spoke in front of another group of people. I faced my biggest fear head on and I got my first standing ovation! That was enough to give me the confidence to keep going, and to accomplish my dream of becoming a professional speaker and a mass-volume salesperson.

It all starts with courage. Courage is about taking action. It requires discipline, vitality and guts to face the tasks you feel uncomfortable about. For example, in sales, accepting a "no" isn't an act of courage unless a "no" bothers you. Courage belongs to every salesperson who faces an inner fear. It is deciding to deal with your fear that takes courage.

What a shame that we are sometimes so overwhelmed by our fears that we can't see that our finest characteristic is about to take us to new heights . . . and its name is courage.

Here are some quotations on the topic of fear. When I need courage to face fear, I review these. You may want to refer to these quotes when you are held back because of fear.

Do the thing you fear most and you will control fear.

Bobby Charleton

Do the thing you fear to do and keep doing it; that is the quickest and surest way ever discovered to conquer fear.

Dale Carnegie

We have nothing to fear but fear itself.

Franklin D. Roosevelt

Courage is not the absence of fear, but rather the judgment that something is more important than fear.

Ambrose Redbone

It is the mind that maketh good of ill, that maketh wretch or happy, rich or poor.

Edmund Spenser

Worry is a state of mind based upon fear. It paralyzes one's reasoning faculty, destroys self-confidence and initiative.

Napoleon Hill

Failure will never overtake you if your determination to succeed is strong enough.

Og Mandino

I would rather be a failure in something that I love than a success in something that I didn't.

George Burns

Our greatest glory is not in never failing, but in rising every time we fall.

Confucius

Develop success from failures. Discouragement and failure are two of the secret stepping stones to success.

Dale Carnegie

In summary, one of the things we fear most is failure. You must realize, though, that you learn from failure. You can overcome the fear of failure by giving yourself permission to fail. Keep in mind that success is based on good judgment and good judgment is based on experience. And how does one get experience? Right—through trial and failure.

Failure is not easy to accept. You need to be able to see the good behind every experience in life. Rather than criticizing yourself, recognize the things that were done right, the effort of trying and the lessons learned.

You will need courage, because the only way to eliminate fear is to face it head on. Have courage and develop self-confidence through the elimination of fear. You can do it!

The first and best victory is to conquer self. To be conquered by self is, of all things, the most shameful and vile.

Plato

3. You have the right to ask.

Ask and it shall be given you; seek and ye shall find; knock and it shall be opened unto you. For every one that asketh receiveth;

and he that seeketh, findeth; and to him that knocketh it shall be opened.

Luke 11: 9-10

If we don't ask for something, how are we ever going to get it? By simply not asking, we receive an automatic "no" answer. But is that not the reason we don't ask? We don't want to be rejected. Understand what was said above—you don't ask, you don't get. When you do ask, do you not increase your chances of getting a yes? You already know that the worst answer you can get is a no. Therefore, why not ask and increase your chances of getting a yes. Make it a habit to ask, but be careful what you ask for because you may get it!

Imagine the salesperson who doesn't ask questions in order to understand the prospect's needs or to ask for the order. Picture the person who doesn't ask for the promotion, the person who doesn't ask for a hand in marriage. Do they get what they want? Don't ever be too shy to ask. What is the worst response you can get? "No." So what have you lost? You can't lose something you never had. Now, imagine you ask the same question and the answer is yes, just for asking. How much further ahead would you be now?

If I hadn't asked my wife Joan to go to the high school graduation with me I might never have found that wonderful and loving partner. If I hadn't asked my friend John for a loan, we might not have been able to build our first home, nor been able to live in our dream home of today. If I hadn't asked for guidance, I likely wouldn't have received it. And if I hadn't asked myself what I wanted out of life, I doubt that I'd be where I (happily) am today.

Ask of yourself, ask of others, and ask often. Don't ever be too shy to ask. If you don't ask, you don't get.

Later, in Section C, you will gain a better appreciation for asking questions and for what asking questions can do for you and your success as a salesperson. For now, just get over the fear of asking. We will shortly deal with the fear of a rejection.

Indeed, the more you ask, the more you get. If you need help, if you want a sale, if you want a referral, if you do not understand something, if you want more out of your profession, what must you do? Ask! You do have the right to ask! Make it a habit to ask. Asking can help you to choose how to use your time and energy most effectively.

4. You have the right to decide how you will use your time and energy.

The whole secret of freedom from anxiety over not having enough time lies not in working more hours, but in the proper planning of the hours.

Frank Bettger

You have a sales job and other responsibilities where there are expectations of you. But who decided to take on these responsibilities? I understand; you needed a job and you had no choice. I've been there. But think about this: is what you are doing bringing you closer to the realization of your success? If so, great! If not, maybe you should reconsider how you are using your time and energy. You have the right to decide how much effort you invest toward achieving your goals. (In Section B, we will discuss time management for sales professionals in greater detail.)

I once worked for a large corporation that had a performance review process. Employees and their supervisors set objectives for the year and reviewed them quarterly. Individuals spent a lot of time and energy on the reviews and appraisals—up to five days a year. This was a great form of discipline, and worth the effort because feedback improves job performance.

But whose performance is being appraised? Is that appraisal, or feedback, an internal or an external process? By the way, who is the most important person in the world? How much time and energy do we provide directly to *that* person and his or her success?

Similarly, as salespeople you claim to spend your time qualifying and understanding the needs of prospects. (Qualifying, as it is used in this book, means determining whether the person has a need, a want, a budget and the capability of making a decision to purchase your product or service.) But I wonder how many of you have taken the time to qualify yourselves and understand the needs of the person you see in the mirror.

How many jobs will you go through to find career happiness? How much time and energy will you invest to discover your own needs and desires? Have you set out an annual or lifetime plan of action? Are you reviewing your performance on a regular basis? Remember, you have the right to decide how you will use your time and energy.

Understanding and believing in these four rights will make a significant difference in your sales success.

The discipline I refer to as #4 in *Online for Life* is **know yourself**. It is the other important discipline to share with you in this section on You—The Bull's Eye Attitude. Here I'll highlight a few important elements of Discipline #4 for you to consider.

> *No person has a chance to enjoy permanent success until he begins to look in a mirror for the real cause of all his mistakes.*
>
> Napoleon Hill

We all bear the influence of our friends, schools, parents—and our total environment. Some of this baggage is positive and some of it is negative. We accept a lot of it as the absolute truth and the way life must be. This has caused us to set our own limitations, most of them externally influenced. But are these things we have learned really true?

If you take the time to know yourself, you become internally driven. Know yourself from the inside out—your values, your motivators and de-motivators, your strengths and your weaknesses. Realize how you see yourself.

As adults we can decide who and what we will and will not be. Take advantage of this power. Your greatest strength and direction will come from inside you, not from the outside world.

We are easily influenced by people and circumstances, and forget sometimes who we really are and what is important to us. These influences can control us and force us into a mold of conformity, diminishing any thought or action that might develop our individuality and creativity.

If we repeatedly hear the words "you can't," it's easy to be convinced that we cannot achieve our sales success. If we hear "anyone who makes a lot of money is a crook," we may be influenced not to make any significant amount of money. On the other hand, a positive message like "anyone who controls their spending can accumulate money" would encourage us to control our spending.

You have the right to select what motivates you and to understand your feelings. The choices you make will direct the course you follow in life.

Over the years I have had the opportunity to complete a variety of profiling tests. These tests can tell participants about their strengths and weaknesses, their personality type and the sorts of work that may suit them. I have learned so much about myself this way that I recommend you take advantage of these opportunities to learn about yourself.

No one is perfect. We all have our strengths and weaknesses—that's human nature. What we need to know is who we are and what our strengths and weaknesses are. This will guide us into doing things we enjoy and avoiding things we don't. We will be able to set and achieve realistic goals. We will live a happy life, a life of our choice.

If you have no concept of who or what you are, your journey into the future will be uncertain and dependent upon circumstances—circumstances that are not all under your control. You will wander aimlessly through life. Without a well-defined identity, your ability to succeed will depend on luck. But success is not about luck. Defining your identity will keep you focused as you set priorities, organize tasks, deal with emergencies and accomplish challenges in your personal and business life.

The first step in defining your identity involves self-awareness—seeing yourself as you really are. It involves being honest with yourself. Taking inventory of yourself can be an uncomfortable and even painful experience, but you must do it in order to move forward.

Who Am I?

Like most people in society today, you probably answered with the roles that you play. We all play a variety of roles in life. Some of the roles that you play or positions you hold in life may be parent, spouse, sales professional, manager . . .

Over the years and in many speaking engagements, I have recommended the following exercise to help participants discover their real "identity." David Sandler goes into great detail with this exercise and the subject of identity in his book *You Can't Teach a Kid to Ride a Bike at a Seminar* (see Bibliography).

Identify and rate your roles from 1 to 10 as to how you see or feel about yourself in each role, 1 being "poor" and 10 being "great."

What You "R" (Roles)	Rating
_____	_____
_____	_____
_____	_____
_____	_____
_____	_____
_____	_____
_____	_____
_____	_____
Average Rating of What You "R"	_____

Who Am I, Without Roles?

When answering the next question, imagine yourself alone, with no roles. Who is this person? Look into the mirror; what do you see? Are you honest, sincere, positive, committed, loving, caring, giving or respectful? Are you jealous, negative, dishonest, humble, uncommitted, disrespectful or living in fear? Try to list as many points about yourself as you can. You can always come back and add to your list. Do your best for now, but do it.

Rate yourself from 1 to 10 on how you see or feel about yourself without your roles, again 1 being "poor" and 10 being "great."

Who You "I" (Identity)	Rating
_____	_____
_____	_____
_____	_____
_____	_____
_____	_____
_____	_____
_____	_____
_____	_____
_____	_____
Average Rating of Who You "I"	_____

Where is your highest rating?

What You "R" _____ or Who You "I" _____

If the highest rating is your role, "R," beware. What you "R" has become your identity. What would happen if you lost your role(s) or position(s) tomorrow? What would your identity be then?

If your "I" rating is higher than your "R" rating, congratulations! You are on the right track. You are approaching life from the inside out, and that is what matters most.

Your identity and how you feel about yourself is most important.

David Sandler states, "You can perform in your roles (R) only in a manner that is consistent with how you see yourself conceptually (I). In other words, your role corresponds to your identity rating, every time."

This means if you see yourself as a 3, you will perform in your roles as a 3. But if you see yourself as a 10, you will perform as a 10. It all starts from the inside and how you see or feel about yourself. That is where your self-esteem and self-confidence come from.

Self-esteem and self-confidence will give you the courage and discipline to do the things you always wanted to do. Lack of self-confidence or self-esteem will cause you to procrastinate, avoid decisions, take few or no risks, and leave life to chance.

Who is the most important person in the world?

_____

What would I like to rate that person as?

A _____ (1 — 10) by _____ (date)

Focus on your "I" — your internal identity. That is where you will experience the greatest of miracles.

Let's now take a look at why so many people have a fear of cold calling. Is it because of an increased chance of rejection? Of course it is. No one likes to be rejected, but if you know how to deal with rejection, it is not a problem. First answer this question for yourself: When you are rejected, is it the role or the identity that is being rejected? If you answered "the role," you are right. The problem arises when we allow role rejection to enter into identity rejection — when we start to take things personally.

That reminds me of the time I went through several interviews for a sales position with IBM many years ago. Each interview was great, except they tried something on the final interview that got me. All along I was asking the right questions and giving the right answers. Then in the final interview they told me they made a decision not to hire me. I was rejected and I took it personally, instead of challenging it. Later, I learned that was part of their selection process — to see how the interviewees dealt with rejection and how we could turn it around into a sale. I failed, but I did learn a valuable lesson.

Imagine how much more productive you would be if you didn't allow fear and rejection to step into your way. The funny thing is, both are a state of mind and we can control our states of mind. Let's take a look at the following diagram to understand how the mind and body work in unison.

Sales Success Programming

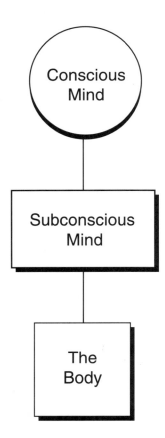

Conscious Mind

- Where ideas are formatted
- Where information is generated through five senses
- Free will resides here
- Pain, pleasure and limitation originate here
- Has ability to accept or reject
- Has ability to dream
- Has ability to concentrate

Subconscious Mind

- The storage center
- No ability to reject
- Must accept every thought your conscious mind chooses to accept
- Will create whatever is necessary to fulfill every idea the conscious mind conceives
- Utilizes all the forces of nature to produce results
- More susceptible to the influence of feelings or emotions

The Body

- An instrument of the mind—it mirrors your thoughts and feelings
- Acts out the behavior and actions that govern your results

You cannot always control circumstances, but you can control your own thoughts.

Charles E. Popplestone

There are things in life that we cannot control, and things that are under our full control. One of the first things we must do is get into the habit of distinguishing which is which. Then we can start to take control of our lives and our destiny.

Each day we go out into the world where we are faced with many external influences that are not part of ourselves, not under our control, and that cause us to react. Influences like the weather, the news, the traffic, the crowds of people or the lack of people, and the comments we hear. When you wake up to a rainy day, rather than a sunny day, do you see things differently? When you get caught in traffic, how do you react? When faced with rejection, or failure, what do you do?

How we react is under our full control. We have that freedom of choice. We can react as favorably to a rainy day as we would to a sunny day, appreciating what good the rain does, or we can complain about the clouds. When we get caught in traffic we can get upset, which does us no good because we cannot control the traffic, or we can use the time to visualize our dreams. When we face rejection we can be discouraged and even quit, or we can seek out the hidden opportunity, knowing that at least we will learn from the experience.

A state of mind cannot be purchased; it must be created. Your states of mind are your thoughts in your conscious mind. You can improve the quality of your life by managing your thoughts, by reframing them so that they empower rather than depress you. As an adult, you have absolute control over your own conscious mind. Your thoughts and the way you deal with them in your conscious mind control your attitude and determine how you react to situations. Your thoughts, should you choose to accept them, are you!

Because you have the ability to control your own state of mind, you can overcome habits and even fears. You have the capability and the right to accept or reject your thoughts. It's called willpower and it exists only in the conscious state.

If you fail to control your own conscious mind, how can you control anything else? Control your thoughts or your thoughts will control you. There is no half-way compromise. Mind control is a result of self-discipline and habit. Keep your mind busy with a definite purpose backed by a definite plan.

Our thought processes and our reactions make the difference in our lives. To take control of our lives we must first identify the things we have no control over as well as the things we do have control over.

Is there any difference between the two? Did you notice that the things that are not under your control are external to you, while the things under your control are internal? This is the source of the only true motivation.

Start by taking control of the things that are under your control. Take a close look at your beliefs and re-evaluate them. You are now an adult and can distinguish between what is real and what is not.

You may have been told something that you accepted as the truth at the time and it became part of your belief system. That belief may have stopped you from doing the things you enjoy or want to do.

For example, many years ago I internalized the belief that to succeed I must go the extra mile. The problem I have is identifying where that mile ends, as moderation is not one of my strengths. This is a belief that I fully support, but at what cost? Recently, I've made the effort to re-evaluate this belief, in search of a degree of moderation and a balanced lifestyle.

You probably have similar baggage. Your assignment is to identify your inappropriate beliefs so you can later create a plan to replace them with appropriate beliefs.

Your beliefs drive your attitude. Your attitude drives everything! Change your beliefs and you change your attitude. Your attitude determines how you feel. How you feel determines how you act. How you act determines your results, all of which are under your control. Are they not?

Let's take a look at your attitude. Do you have an attitude of gratitude? What is your attitude toward yourself? Your attitudes are your thoughts. Do you talk to yourself? What do you say? Is it positive or negative? Are you even aware of what you are saying?

Research tells us that up to 70 percent of our self-talk is negative and that it takes 11 positive statements to reverse one negative thought. That's a lot of work. Your first challenge is to become aware of what you are saying and what you are thinking, as our thoughts of today dictate our reality of tomorrow.

I can remember when I was in my twenties working as a sales representative for a major oil company and doing a lot of driving. I drove so much that I could not help but think about the mileage I was doing. I would say to myself that I was increasing my chances of having a car accident because I drove so much. Well, it wasn't long after focusing on that thought that it became a reality, and I totalled a car. Fortunately, no one was injured.

Today, I realize how I created that thought, reinforced it through negative self-talk and invited it to happen. I also realize that my thoughts and self-talk are 100 percent under my control.

The opposite also applies. Many times before going in on a sales call I would take the time to visualize the visit. I would see myself establishing rapport and trust with the prospect and having them like me. I would see myself taking notes and asking qualifying questions and doing a great presentation. I would see the prospect buying and becoming an ongoing friend and client. This was all visualized in my mind. I set myself up for success. It was a state of mind.

How can you control your state of mind—the things that are under your control?

First you must become aware of what you are saying or thinking. Then you must decide if this is the way you want it to be. If it is, you accept it and move on. If it is not the way you want it to be, reject it. Put a big solid red X through it. Stop it!

You may say something like "I can't." I know, and you know, that with a bit of effort you can have, do or be anything you desire in life. Place, and see, a big solid red X through the words "I cXn't." Stop it as you think of it! That is how you can take control.

Another method you can use is to place an elastic band on your wrist. Every time you have a negative thought or self-talk, pull the band and let it slap you on the wrist. That will send a message to your conscious mind to reject that thought or message.

Be aware of what you are thinking, what you are saying to yourself or how you react to events that are not under your control. Take the time to eliminate those non-supporting thoughts and remarks, and soon you will be rewarded with the self-control required to be a success in sales. All it takes is 21 consecutive days of self-discipline to make it a habit. (See the Monthly Monitor Chart in Section B.)

What about your habits? Are you controlling your habits, or are they controlling you? Negative habits such as self-criticism, procrastination, indecision and fear lead to failure. Negative thoughts prevent us from accomplishing the things we want in life.

Changing your thought process and habits will require a lot of discipline. Discipline involves doing what you have to do, even when you don't want to do it. It means respecting the commitment you made to yourself and doing whatever it takes to get it done, when it needs to be done. This will be your start to taking control of your life through self-discipline.

Many of my behaviors and habits developed over time. I really learned to master discipline by following the prescribed method of reading *The Greatest Salesman in the World* by Og Mandino. I applied the 30-day discipline that eventually made me a slave to some good habits and attitudes.

The prescribed method was to read one of 10 short scrolls, three times a day for 30 days, before proceeding on to the next scroll. If you missed a morning, noon or evening reading, you had to start that scroll over again from day one. It seemed pretty easy, at first.

A book that could have been read in an afternoon took me 18 months to complete, as prescribed. But the results astonished me. What do you think would happen to you if you kept repeating the same positive message to yourself three times a day for 30 days?

Summary

You have the right to like yourself as you are, to fail, to ask and to decide how you will use your time and energy.

Identify who you are, with and without roles.

Keep rejection on the role side and recognize the importance of keeping a high identity.

Review programming for sales success through the conscious mind to the subconscious and to the body.

To make a decision, take control of your attitude, thoughts and self-talk using the red X to control negativity.

Your beliefs determine your attitudes, your attitude determines your feelings, your feelings then determine your actions, and your actions determine your results.

A2 • Your Bull's Eye Attitude Toward Your Organization

In section A1 you took the time to get to know the most important person in the world, located at the core of the target. Belief in yourself is a must, as no one else will believe in you if you don't first believe in yourself. But then there are other components that you also have to believe in when you are in sales. The next ring on the target is your attitude and your level of belief toward your organization.

You may feel really good about yourself and know that you are the best person for the sales job you hold, but for some reason, you don't fully believe in your organization, product or service or the team you work with. You know as well as I do that your attitude and level of belief will be transparent to the client and that a sale will not take place because of it. In turn you may externalize and blame the organization for a poor product or service, poor delivery times or service. Yet who is the real problem here? Not only do you need a strong belief system in place for yourself, you need one for the organization, its products and services and the team you represent. If one element is not strong, you will lose the sale. So how do you deal with this problem?

Well, there are two ways. One is to communicate and solve the problem or understand the circumstances surrounding the problem such that your belief system improves. The other is to leave the organization and find one that you do believe in strongly.

When we talk about belief in an organization we ask about your organization's mission statement: Do you buy into it? Why? Why not? Does your attitude reflect your belief in the mission statement? Do you see the sales team's attitude reflecting their belief in the mission statement? Do you see the entire organizational team's attitude reflecting their belief in the mission statement? Do you feel that the following support the organization toward the attainment of the mission statement internally and externally: Training, Communications, Image, Marketing, Networking, other?

Imagine an organization trying to navigate without everyone rowing in the same direction. Salespeople are the front line in most organizations. Salespeople usually know the most about the organization they represent and their products and services. They also know the most about the organization's clients and potential prospects. If salespeople are not fully comfortable with what and who they are representing, they can do more harm than good.

Consider the following questions:

As a salesperson, how do you feel about your organization on a scale of 0 to 10?

Poor — — — — — — — — — — — — — — — — — Great
0   1   2   3   4   5   6   7   8   9   10

Why?_____

As a salesperson, how do you feel about your organization's products and services?

Poor — — — — — — — — — — — — — — — — — Great
0   1   2   3   4   5   6   7   8   9   10

Why?_____

Are you a team player? If so, how? If not, why not?
As a salesperson, how do you feel about your fellow team members?

Poor — — — — — — — — — — — — — — — — — Great
0   1   2   3   4   5   6   7   8   9   10

Why?_____

Based on your responses to the previous questions, you either strongly believe in the organization, its products and services and team members that you represent, or you have some work to do to get it up there. If you don't do something about it, you should consider leaving, as you will be your biggest problem.

Let me share a personal example with you. I was a door-to-door salesman for a home fire alarm system company. This is when home fire alarms first came into being in the mid-1970s. I believed in myself, the organization, its products and the team that I represented. I worked hard and I did well. Within six months, I overheard in a conversation that the organization I represented was being sued because the fire alarm system that we sold did not go off during a fire and someone almost died.

I didn't understand why my sales dropped then, but I do understand today. I was still working hard, but my belief in the reliability of the product fell. I found it difficult to sell something I no longer believed in. I addressed it with the team, but they found me to be negative. Within a short period of time I left the organization and started selling something I did believe in. Isn't it funny how we succeed when we have a strong belief in something?

Belief is the key. If the business you are working in became yours, or if you became self-employed (100 percent commission) doing what you are doing, what would you do differently?

I refer to this as having an owner's mentality. Do you have an owner's mentality toward your job, and your organization? If you are proactive you probably do. However, if you are reactive you probably don't, as you are waiting for someone to tell you what to do.

No matter what business you are in, you should always treat it as if it were your own business, particularly when it comes to sales. When you are proactive you are in control. Life is always easier when you are one step ahead of management, or the client. Consider what an owner's mentality can do for you and your organization. It is not too late to get started.

Summary

Reflect, confirm and take hold of your attitude toward your organization, its products and services and fellow team members.

Develop an owner's mentality by being proactive.

A3 • Your Bull's Eye Attitude Toward Your Market

In section A1 you took the time to get to know the most important person in the world located at the core of the target. Then we discussed the next ring on the target—your attitude and your level of belief toward your organization. Now we will look at that outer ring—your attitude and your level of belief toward your market.

In order to be successful in sales we must believe in all three components of the Bull's Eye Attitude—you, your organization and your market.

The first question here is, can your market support your products and services? If it can, great. But if you don't think the market can, guess what? You're right and your results will show it. You will be better to give up and find a new market for your products and services or a new product or service that will fit that market.

I used to sell recreational real estate in West Quebec. I was quite successful at it. I believed in me, the organizations I represented—Campeau Corporation, Cadillac-Fairview and Mont Cascades Developments—and, for a long time, in the market I was selling to.

However, with a separatist government elected in Quebec, the market changed. The market consisted of English Canadians from Ottawa. They stopped purchasing West Quebec real estate because of the fear of what would happen to their investment if Quebec separated from Canada. Real estate values in West Quebec plummeted, as did my commissions and my belief in the market. I hung in far too long. I believed the market would change, but to date—25 years later—it hasn't. In the meantime, I have moved on to bigger and better things. Maybe you should too if you don't believe there is a market for your products or services.

The market perception of salespeople can be an issue too. How does your market perceive salespeople? How does your market perceive you?

How would you like them to perceive you? What are you doing about it? Keep in mind that your market is what makes your living. You have to react to their needs and desires.

In the case of real estate transactions, I was never licensed. There was no need to be as I was not selling private lots or homes. I was representing major land developers and builders. Real estate agents did not have a good reputation at the time. They were battling with each other over commissions and it was a dog-eat-dog business. I wanted nothing to do with it, and deliberately stayed away from that end of the business. It was a good thing that I did, too. Most of them went under during the early eighties, while I survived because of my consultative and customized approach.

So how are you positioned in your market? Are you getting the respect you deserve or are you just like the rest of them? In order to stand out from the crowd you have to create your own personal marketing program. I am not talking about the marketing program created by your organization, I am talking about a personal marketing program—one built by you for you.

One of the greatest opportunities we have in sales is to develop our reputation and to build our network. Some of us are even paid to do just that. With or without a sale, each and every day we are building, or destroying, our reputation and our network. The key is to build that reputation and network through a personal marketing program.

People buy from people, particularly people they like. A personal marketing program will separate you from everyone else. You can position yourself as the leader in the field with the most credibility and respect, if you are willing to go the extra mile. The extra mile is simply giving more of your expertise in a manner that is valued.

But first take the time to define your market. Who are they; what do they look like; where are they located; what are their problems, their needs and desires? Describe your ideal prospect—profile them. Describe your ideal customer—profile them. What are their likes and dislikes? How do you market to them? How do you meet them? How do you start and maintain a relationship?

Your marketing department has probably already asked the above questions, but you need to answer them for yourself based on your knowledge. You are the product or service now and you need your own marketing program. People buy whatever you have to sell because of who you are. How do you need to position yourself in the marketplace—your territory or your accounts?

There are some simple and obvious ways to position yourself for success in your personal marketing program. For example, you can identify the associations that your market gets involved in and you too can get actively involved in a leadership or executive role within that association. I have even gone as far as being a founding president of an association chapter.

If it is credibility that you need, consider writing a newsletter, articles or tip sheets for local newspapers or magazines on a regular basis or share your expertise through public speaking. I do both of these on a regular basis. I have articles that have been published worldwide with my photo and contact information. In addition, every time I speak I get more leads for speaking, sales training and education materials. The more articles I write and the more I speak, the more I sell. Think of what would happen to your sales if you publicly shared your information in a passionate and sincere way.

The objective behind your personal marketing plan is to position *you* as an expert in your field, as someone who is known, recognized and networked. With a good personal marketing plan you will be referred and chased through word of mouth as opposed to having to chase. But you must also keep your network in mind and continually recognize and reward them for their positive behavior. You should even create a win/win referral system as part of your plan.

We have discussed belief in your market, positioning, personal marketing plan and your reputation and network. It all sounds good, but you are not the only one in the market. You probably have some competitors.

Just as you profiled your ideal prospect and customer, you must also know your competition inside out if you want to position yourself for success. On the following pages you will find a list of items that you should consider when completing a competitive analysis.

It is essential that you have a clear understanding of your competitive advantages in your target market. By knowing your strengths and weaknesses, and those of your competition, you can be in an advantage position.

Your job would then be to develop your competitive advantage statement, a statement that is unique to your products or services. Keep it short and to the point.

Competitive Analysis

Rate your organization and your main competitors on a scale of 0 to 10, 0 being low and 10 being high, in the following areas. After completing this analysis, prioritize in the "Important" column, 12 of these items to be looked at immediately.

	Us	A	B	C	Important
		Competitors			
Product/Service quality	___	___	___	___	_____
Product/Service selection	___	___	___	___	_____
Product/Service depth	___	___	___	___	_____
Unique product/Service	___	___	___	___	_____
Availability	___	___	___	___	_____
Product/Service price	___	___	___	___	_____
Guarantees/Warrantees	___	___	___	___	_____
Packaging	___	___	___	___	_____
Unit of measure (e.g., doz.)	___	___	___	___	_____
Name brands	___	___	___	___	_____
Generic brands	___	___	___	___	_____
Sales force	___	___	___	___	_____
Sales methods	___	___	___	___	_____
Advertising	___	___	___	___	_____
Promotions	___	___	___	___	_____
Methods of distribution	___	___	___	___	_____
Length of time in business	___	___	___	___	_____

Credit policies   ___ ___ ___ ___ _____

Market position   ___ ___ ___ ___ _____

Image/Reputation   ___ ___ ___ ___ _____

Innovativeness   ___ ___ ___ ___ _____

Special skills   ___ ___ ___ ___ _____

Special knowledge   ___ ___ ___ ___ _____

Available capital   ___ ___ ___ ___ _____

Available credit   ___ ___ ___ ___ _____

Credit for clients   ___ ___ ___ ___ _____

Financial control   ___ ___ ___ ___ _____

Management expertise   ___ ___ ___ ___ _____

Systems and controls   ___ ___ ___ ___ _____

Strategic planning   ___ ___ ___ ___ _____

Parking   ___ ___ ___ ___ _____

Training   ___ ___ ___ ___ _____

Research and development ___ ___ ___ ___ _____

Network/Contacts   ___ ___ ___ ___ _____

Quality of people   ___ ___ ___ ___ _____

Visual merchandising   ___ ___ ___ ___ _____

Location   ___ ___ ___ ___ _____

Other:

_____   ___ ___ ___ _____

_____   ___ ___ ___ _____

_____   ___ ___ ___ _____

_____   ___ ___ ___ _____

Note your differences and use them to your advantage.

Summary

Reflect, confirm and take hold of your attitude toward the market.

Identify the who, what, where and how's of your market.

Profile your ideal prospect/customer.

Develop a personal marketing plan to position yourself as the expert in your market.

Gain a better understanding of your competition.

Congratulations! You have now completed Section A—Attitude, the first and most important step, the foundation of the ABC, 123 Sales Results System.

Section A • The Bull's Eye Attitude

Lessons Learned: _____

_____

_____

I Commit to Implement:

1. _____

_____

2. _____

_____

3. _____

_____

I Need to Work on:

1. _____

_____

2. _____

_____

Section B

• • •

Bull's Eye Behavior:
Targeting Your Sales Effort

Bull's Eye Behaviour: Targeting Your Sales Effort

In this section we are going to discuss behavior. Behavior is the manner in which you conduct yourself, the way you act, function or react. The 1,2,3's are the goals and behaviors from a personal, organizational and market targeting level. Without goals there is no reason to do anything, no motivation to take daily actions or go the extra mile.

Appropriate behavior drives opportunities as you learn to target your sales efforts. Opportunities come from setting goals, written S.M.A.R.T. goals. What do you want out of life or out of your business? Who can determine this for you and who can make it happen? What are the daily behaviors that you must apply to live the life of your dreams?

It is those daily behaviors, and learning when to implement them, that will make a big difference in your level of sales success. For example, as salespeople we need to constantly network, call on prospects, qualify them, present, help them buy and follow up with them. When is the best time to be conducting these behaviors? Once you identify these behaviors and times and stick to them, watch your time management skills and results improve dramatically.

Now let's take a look at your market. Do you know where the bulk of your business is coming from? Can you clearly define the clients? Do you have a good handle on who you should be targeting in on—that is, if you want a maximum return on your investment in time? Then as you target in, are you in a position to obtain pertinent industry, organizational and client information?

All of these behaviors will be discussed in the following pages. But before we proceed, let's go back to the core of the target—you.

B1 • Why You Come to Work—Setting Personal Goals

Behavior, like attitude, starts with you. What you do for a living is a choice you've made. But there is a reason you've made that choice and that choice goes beyond making money. Sure, money has something to do with it, but it is not the money that gets you out of bed in the morning—it is what you want to do with the money that keeps you motivated. It is the realization of your dreams, and dreams can be realized when you take the time to organize, plan and put your plan into action.

One of the greatest learning experiences I have had working in sales was realizing how we were always setting sales targets and objectives, and being measured against them. This is a good practice and keeps us focused on our sales targets. So why not apply those same goal-setting and monitoring strategies to our personal lives so that we too can stay focused on our dreams and end up where we want to be?

Today, in most organizations, management devotes enormous energy to setting work objectives and conducting performance reviews for individual employees. Corporations go through this time-consuming and costly exercise to ensure the most favorable results for their firm.

In professions such as ours (sales), we spend considerable time questioning, listening, discovering and understanding the needs of clients in order to provide a recommended solution or action plan.

In contrast, how much time and energy do you expend discovering your own needs and desires, and then consciously setting objectives, developing action plans with measurable performance standards, and finally reviewing your own performance? By engaging in such an exercise, you will be doing something about your life. You will be going to work on yourself, for yourself. This is where real changes in behavior have to start.

Once again, I refer you to *Online for Life: The 12 Disciplines for Living Your Dreams*. The exercises in Disciplines #5, #6 and #7 will help you to discover your dreams, organize them into a sense of priority and help you to determine if you are prepared to pay the price to make those dreams a reality.

For the purpose of this book, and your professional sales career, I will share Discipline #8 with you. In Discipline #8 we learn how to set goals and create a goal logbook. The process, once you learn how to use it for yourself, is the same for setting your sales and career goals. Unlike organizations who want us to do it for them, I want you to do it for you.

Are you ready to commit yourself to developing personal goals, making plans and taking action accordingly?

Yes _____   No _____

If yes, sign here: _____

Success is the progressive realization of worthwhile goals.

Earl Nightingale

When you believe in your dreams, nothing but self-imposed limitations will stop you from achieving them. Your first step is to define your dreams as goals. A goal is a specific and measurable result that must be achieved within specified time, resource and cost constraints. A goal is an end, a result, and not just a task to be performed. It describes the condition we want to achieve. Our goals guide our actions and help us plan at work and at home. When we focus on our goals, long- and short-range, our present is determined by our future . . . not our past.

Visualize your first goal. Clearly understand your destination. Now the steps you take will all be in the right direction. You can examine each part of your life in the context of what really matters to you. Your goals are an extension of your values.

Goal setting is the process you use to select, define and put into operation the expectations you have for yourself.

Why set goals? What's in it for you?

Goal setting focuses your efforts and improves your direction in life.

Goal setting causes you to set priorities and become more organized.

Goal setting turns your wishful thinking into reality.

Goal setting points out to you your successes as you achieve them, motivating you on to further success.

Goal setting can improve your self-esteem.

Goal setting makes you responsible for your own life. It causes you to define your own value system.

Goal setting makes you aware of your strengths, which you can use to overcome obstacles and solve problems.

Goal setting points out your weaknesses. You can begin setting new goals to improve in those areas and turn them into strengths.

Record keeping is important. Writing down your goals and action plans represents a commitment. Otherwise your dreams are merely wishful thinking. You can reread and visualize written goals. They are credible and legitimate. They live and lead you onward. When you write you have begun to act. Inertia is gone. You sense accomplishment already.

How should you phrase your goals? Goals must be S.M.A.R.T.— Specific, Measurable, Attainable, Relevant and Trackable to a timetable. Let's look at each of these elements in detail.

S. Goals must be Specific. "Happiness" or "success" are too vague. Ask yourself: What exactly do I want to do, be or have? For example, let's say you are getting too close to weighing 200 pounds and you want to reduce to 185 pounds within six months. You could write: In order to be healthier and more energetic, I will lose 14 pounds within the next six months, starting today, and maintain a weight of 185 pounds from that point on.

M. Is your goal Measurable? How will you know you have achieved your goal?

A. Is it Attainable? Give yourself a chance to succeed. Take little steps and succeed. Success breeds success.

R. Is it Relevant? Would the attainment of the goal be worthwhile to you? Before you can answer this question you need to know what kind of life you want.

T. Is there a way of Tracking your performance on a timetable? How do you know you are getting closer to your goal? Select dates when you will measure your progress against the milestones in your plan. You will either re-affirm that you are on track or make adjustments.

Consider the following as you set each goal:

Is this goal really mine? Am I doing this for myself or somebody else? If you are doing it for somebody else, you are not living a life of your choosing.

Is it morally right and fair?

Are my short-range goals consistent with my long-range goals? Keep in mind where you want to be 10 to 20 years from now.

Can I commit myself to completing the project? If not, don't set yourself up for failure and disappointment. Save the goal for a time in your life when you can commit to making the effort.

Can I visualize myself reaching this goal? If you can't see it, it won't happen. Henry Ford said it best: "Whether you think you can or you think you can't, you're absolutely right."

State the Goal

When you know what your specific objectives are concerning your distant, immediate and intermediate goals, you will be more apt to recognize that which will help you achieve them.

W. Clement Stone

Take a moment now and write out one of your goals on the sample "goal log" page at the end of this chapter. You can also complete the exercises on blank sheets of paper.

Once you have it written out, review it to see if the goal is S.M.A.R.T. Remember, to be S.M.A.R.T. it must be specific (well defined or described) measurable, attainable, realistic and trackable (to a specific date).

I remember doing a workshop and a participant had the following goal: "to build a chalet by May." I asked if she felt it was S.M.A.R.T.? The group started to analyze her goal. They all started to ask her questions about size, exterior and interior finish, location and more. Before long that goal was revised to: "to build and move into a 1500-square-meter luxury post-and-beam chalet featuring hardwood floors, low maintenance and a southern exposure toward the ski hills at Mont Tremblant, Quebec, by May 30, 2000." It could have been even more specific, but this made the goal much clearer.

Be as descriptive as possible. Understand or define the meaning of each word used. You want to create as clear a picture as you possibly can in as few words as possible.

Date for Completion

From the first day in hospital I had set myself goals. I had promised myself I would be out of that Stryker bed for my birthday, August 26, and I was.

Rick Hansen

The next step is to add a completion date for each of your goals. Be the master of those dates, not the slave. Don't abandon your goals; just change the deadlines if you have to. Self-motivation and personal leadership include the ability to distinguish between defeat and setback.

Turn to your "goal log" pages now and write in a realistic deadline for your goal. You will lay out the milestones toward these dates later in your action plan.

Outcomes

Chance favors the prepared mind.

Louis Pasteur

The outcome is the result you want, expressed in detail. State your outcomes in positive, sensory-based terms: the sights, sounds and feelings you want to experience. For example, look at the weight-reduction goal: "Within six months, I will weigh 185 pounds. I see myself slimmer, my clothes fit better, and I am more attractive. I hear the opening of the storage box of clothes that had gotten too tight, people giving me compliments on my weight, saying how good I look and asking me how I did it. I feel energized, healthy and active."

Take a few moments now and imagine four things you will see, hear and feel when you have completed your goal. Write them in the goal log.

Possible Obstacles

Obstacles are those frightful things you see when you take your eyes off your goal.

Henry Ford

The next task is to identify the obstacles that could stand in your way. What events or circumstances might make it difficult to reach your goal? How will you handle those roadblocks? It is better to identify them now and have alternate plans ready than to be caught by surprise.

Take the time now to list all the obstacles that you might encounter. Once you have done this for each of your goals, go back and prepare your contingency plans. "If this happened, I would . . . " Be ready.

Allow me to share an incident that occurred in my life that led me to identify obstacles and contingency plans in advance on all of my goals.

Just before turning 30, I was employed with Canada's second largest land developer and experiencing a high level of success. I was responsible for over 10,000 acres of commercial, industrial and residential land in the National Capital Region. I also sold a lot of their land in Aylmer and Gatineau, Quebec. I was the only one selling at the time. It got to the point where licensed real estate agents reported me to the Quebec Real Estate Board. I was investigated and learned a lot about what is allowed and what is not. The conclusion was that as long as I was selling land for a developer, I didn't need a real estate license.

Within weeks Canada's largest land developer approached me to ask if I would consider selling for them too. They suggested I leave and take on a contract with my existing employer and with them. I had always wanted to be in business for myself and I figured this would be the time, as we had only one young child. I approached my employer and obtained their support.

So I left the security of the corporate world to go into business for myself, selling residential lots in West Quebec. Both of Canada's largest land developers and builders were getting out of the new-house construction market in the early 1980s. Real estate just wasn't selling. Interest rates were at an all-time high and a separatist government was in power in Quebec.

Immediately after going into business for myself, I started on a plan. The plan was to prepare the lots for a mass sale six weeks before an upcoming provincial election. During the period preceding the sale, I had the lots bulldozed, picketed and signed with lot numbers, dimensions and phone numbers.

Finally, the time arrived. I expected big results, and being the proactive guy that I am, I started to investigate commercial land development opportunities. The marketing kicked in, as did the support from the local media. Within five days, I had sold over 100 individual lots and earned just over $80,000 in commissions. Not a bad week after being in business for only six months.

Having expected this to happen, I had exercised an option to purchase some commercial land and I went to work on it immediately. I was creating a major tourist attraction, and spent $100,000 within the next 20 days preparing the site.

By the time 30 days rolled around, suppliers were looking for money. I was wondering what had happened to mine. I called the office of Canada's largest land developer. There was no answer. I drove into town and visited their office, only to learn that it was closed down and everyone I knew had been let go. I would have to direct my inquiries to a vice-president located in head office in Toronto.

Before long, I met with that VP. After hearing me out, he said he liked me and would give me $5,000. Otherwise, go play in the traffic. He felt he wasn't obliged to pay me because I was not a licensed real estate agent. I could not believe what he was saying. I decided to refuse his offer and seek legal advice based on the experience I had gained from being previously investigated.

Because of a very simple obstacle that could have been identified in advance (with a contingency plan put in place), my "success" became a nightmare.

All five goals that were well in line for accomplishment experienced a major setback. First, I was obliged to pay my suppliers. I went to the local bank and borrowed $10,000 at a 22 percent interest rate. In the end I had borrowed ten $10,000 loans at 22 percent interest. My mortgage came up for renewal at 19 percent, and my lawyer advised me to give him $25,000 up front for court costs or move out of our dream home and into an apartment in Ottawa to avoid Ontario Supreme Court costs. That hurt the most. My wife Joan was pregnant with our second child and was looking forward to raising our children at home. We moved out, rented out our home and found an apartment in town.

It wasn't long after that, I had no choice but to close down the business I had started. I was now in significant debt. Fortunately I landed a job and slowly began to rebuild. Within three years, Canada's largest land developer settled out of court and I secured all monies due to me. I got myself back on my feet again, and ended up in a better position because of the experience.

However, there was no need to go through what I went through, if I had only addressed one possible obstacle: what if they decide not to pay me? Had I even thought of it, I would have waited for the money to be in my hands before proceeding into further investment. That would have been my contingency plan.

Mind you, I do have a "do it now" attitude and don't usually take the time to think about everything that can go wrong. I learn by doing and adjusting as need be. You don't want to think about obstacles for too long, because it will delay you in your actions. Identify the most obvious and potentially most serious ones that come to mind and move on.

Contingency Plans

Success comes to those who set goals and pursue them regard-
less of obstacles and disappointments.

Napoleon Hill

Based on the possible obstacles you have identified, what can you do
in advance to prepare? If that obstacle caught you by surprise it could
knock you down. If you have a contingency plan, you will stand tall and
recognize it as just a bump along the road to success. You implement your
contingency plan and move on. You just saved yourself two steps in the
process—one being knocked down and the other getting back up. Don't
let it take three years out of your life as it did to me.

Take the time now to identify some possible contingency plans to
obstacles you identified earlier.

Skills and Behaviors Required

Almost every goal you set for yourself involves learning. The
ability to learn what you need to know, in a hurry, is the basic
tool for getting what you want.

Joyce Brothers

What skills will you require in order to achieve your goal? How, where
and when will you learn those skills?

Behavior can be defined as the way you conduct yourself. Will you
need to change your behavior in order to put your skills into action?

For example, when we laid out our goal to build our dream home, I
needed to acquire some design and construction skills. Not so much the
"to do" skills but rather an understanding of them in order to negotiate
and inspect the hired skills. So I made it a goal to take a course on building your own home, which turned out to be invaluable.

I developed my behaviors, too. I researched designs and materials. I
read up on things, spoke to many contractors, and made sure I was on top

of everything. I learned how to accept criticism from and provide constructive feedback to the tradesmen, maintain a positive attitude, and persist until the job got done.

People, Groups or Resources Required

> *In order to reach your ultimate goal, you must form a group of people with ambitions like your own, but differing in specialized knowledge. Together, the group can solve problems that no one person alone could solve.*

Napoleon Hill

You can accomplish only so much on your own. You can achieve much more by calling on the help of different people, groups or resources. Regardless of your goal, you will attain it with much less difficulty if you ally yourself with others. Some people create mastermind groups, others create an advisory board, others consult with their friends and families, while others benefit from membership in an association. Through others we sometimes get our best ideas. The best results come from an organized effort of two or more people working toward a definite outcome.

What individuals or groups of people could help you? What resources can you call on? List them now.

For example, while completing the log for my goal to become a speaker, I wanted to become part of a professional speaking association, so I joined the Canadian Association of Professional Speakers. I felt I needed an individual to help fast-track me into the business, internationally. The timing was right and I found Denis Cauvier, right in my own town. When I looked for a speech coach to provide me with constructive feedback, I found Velma Latmore, a person who has dedicated her life to effective communications through Toastmasters. I also needed resource material, so I reorganized my office and got out all the books that had inspired me over the years. I began researching using the Internet and visiting bookstores regularly.

Action Plan

Say three times, "This one thing I do," emphasizing the word one.
One step at a time will get you there much more surely than hap-
hazardly leaping and jumping. It is the steady pace, the consistent
speed that leads to the most efficient start to your destination.

Dr. Norman Vincent Peale

An action plan is a step-by-step outline of the tasks that lead to the achievement of a goal. Treat each action step as a sub-goal.

What do you need to do to turn your goals into reality? Establish a logical sequence of steps. Prioritize them and place a target date for accomplishment beside each activity. By dating each step along the way you can monitor and measure your progress and reward yourself accordingly.

Acknowledge the events beyond your control upon which goal results depend. Identify the areas where you will co-ordinate your actions with other people, in order to get the support you need, when you need it.

Identifying the actions you need to take, and the schedule for those actions, makes all the difference between a wish and a realistic, achievable goal. The main objective is to set up your action plan in a way that guarantees you success. By this I mean create an action plan that is full of little steps taken one at a time so that you can experience success along the way. Too many people just identify gigantic steps, steps that turn out to be unrealistic or unachievable in the time frames allocated. They soon sense that they can't do it and then give up. Don't do that to yourself.

Create an action plan that is set up for success. Little steps at a time. Experience your success on a daily basis. You can't realize your tomorrow's dream without first taking a small step forward today toward its realization.

For example, 20 years ago I laid out a three-phase action plan to build a waterfront home for my family. The first phase was to learn about the local real estate. Over the first 10 to 15 years I acquired a good understanding of land, and when river-front properties finally became available I found the perfect lot.

The next phase was to pay off and prepare the land. Over a period of five years I cleared the trees, put in the driveway, fixed the shoreline, built a boathouse, and put in a septic bed, a flower garden and grass. The property was ready. The only thing missing was the house.

The third and concluding phase (the last two years) was to design the house, sell our old home, acquire the financing and build. One step at a time, we accomplished a dream that went back 20 years.

Take the time now to list all the necessary steps to accomplish each of your goals. Use extra paper if you need it. This is the most important stage in creating your goal log. Take the time to list everything that comes to mind. When you are done, review your list and identify the steps in order of priority. Spend a lot of time in this area before moving on. Identify everything right down to the little steps and set yourself up for success.

Methods of Monitoring and Measuring Progress

> *Goals are not only absolutely necessary to motivate us. They are essential to really keep us alive.*
>
> Robert H. Schuller

Knowing how you're doing will motivate you to keep going. How will you monitor your behavior and measure your progress? Think of some ways in which you can do this on an ongoing basis. Monitoring will allow you to recognize your progress and reward yourself accordingly. It will also warn you to take corrective action should you find you are not following your plan.

How can you make sure you are on track? What sort of measurements can you take regularly? Fill in that part of your goal log now.

At the end of the next section, "What You Expect to Achieve at Work," I will provide you with a simple chart that you can use to monitor your progress.

The Reward (What's in it for me?)

> *I feel the greatest reward for doing is the opportunity to do more.*
>
> Jonas Salk

How are you going to reward yourself when you accomplish your goal? You deserve something besides the achievement of that goal. Visualize the rewards you'll give yourself. Also, decide how you can pay yourself along the way. It will be easier to keep up the good work when you periodically reward yourself.

What are the things you really enjoy? Plan to treat yourself to some of these things after you complete each action step. This way you will practice discipline—doing what you have to do even when you don't want to—and accomplish your goals at the same time. Remember that action that gets rewarded gets repeated.

For example, I like to play golf with clients on Friday afternoons. I usually take some time on Sunday evenings to plan out my week in relation to my monthly goals. I identify the times during the week when I have family and business commitments, and then I fill in my schedule with activities that will help me reach my goals for that month. Before long my schedule is full. By the time Friday rolls around, I either reward myself by playing golf, because I did everything I indicated that I would, or I punish myself and stay in the office and do everything that I didn't do.

Imagine if I rewarded myself for something I indicated that I would do, but then didn't do. Do you think I would have a good game of golf? I don't think so. I would be feeling guilty. However, imagine how well I would play golf, and how much more I would enjoy the game, if it were a reward for doing what I indicated to myself that I would do.

You can use dinners, movies, vacations, clothes, events or whatever you enjoy as rewards. Tie the required disciplines to something you really enjoy and treat these enjoyments as a reward for doing what you indicated you would do. Stop treating yourself to these enjoyments for absolutely no reason, and you will soon be a master of discipline.

Discipline is the key. Discipline is a commitment to yourself to do what you have to do, even when you don't want to do it. As discipline gets recognized and rewarded it gets repeated and becomes a matter of habit.

Commitment

There is not much use climbing the ladder part way. People who succeed have the single-minded devotion to their goal that is best described as total commitment. They have the ability and desire to work to top capacity.

Joyce Brothers

This is where you make a commitment to yourself. This is such an important step that I have dedicated Discipline #9 in *Online for Life* to it.

Goal Log

Creation date: _____   Last updated date: _____

Identify goal: _____

_____

Deadline/Date: _____

Outcome:

What will I see when I get there?

1. _____

2. _____

3. _____

What sounds will I hear?

1. _____

2. _____

3. _____

What will I feel?

1. _____

2. _____

3. _____

Possible obstacles / Contingency plan _____

_____

_____

_____

Skills and behaviors required _____

_____

_____

_____

_____

Identify people, groups or resources required _____

_____

_____

_____

Action Plan with Dates

Action # 1 _____

Start: _____   *Finish:* _____

Action # 2 _____

Start: _____   *Finish:* _____

Action # 3 _____

Start: _____   *Finish:* _____

Action # 4 _____

Start: _____   *Finish:* _____

Action # 5 _____

Start: _____   *Finish:* _____

Action # 6 _____

Start: _____   *Finish:* _____

Action # 7 _____

Start: _____   *Finish:* _____

Action # 8 _____

Start: _____   *Finish:* _____

Action # 9 _____

Start: _____   *Finish:* _____

Action # 10 _____

Start: _____   *Finish:* _____

Action # 11 _____

Start: _____   *Finish:* _____

Action # 12 _____

Start: _____   *Finish:* _____

Methods of monitoring and measuring progress _____

_____

_____

_____

_____

Reward: What's in it for me? _____

_____

_____

_____

I have committed myself to the accomplishment of this goal by:

_____

Signature: _____   Date: _____

Summary

Why do you come to work?—question the answer.

A goal is an end, a result, not just a task to be performed.

Goals are an extension of your values.

Goals must be S.M.A.R.T.—Specific, Measurable, Attainable, Relevant and Trackable to a timetable.

Ask yourself: Is this goal really mine? Is it morally right and fair? Are my short-range goals consistent with my long-range goals? Can I commit myself to completing the project? Can I visualize myself reaching this goal?

Create a goal logbook and address each of the following areas:

- State the goal, date for completion and outcomes expressed in sensory-based terms—the sights, sounds and feelings you want to experience.

- Identify obstacles you might meet; develop the contingency plans to overcome those possible obstacles; identify the skills and behaviors you'll need, and the people, groups or resources you can call on for help.

- Develop a detailed step-by-step success-oriented action plan with start and finish dates, and with a method of monitoring and measuring your progress.

- Create a system to recognize and reward yourself for doing what you indicated you would do along the way.

- Finally, make a commitment to yourself to follow through and do what you have to do.

B2 • What You Expect to Achieve at Work
—Setting Business Goals

Now that you know how to set goals and create a goal log for yourself, it should be a lot easier for you to go through the same process with your objectives at work. As I mentioned earlier, in most organizations, management devotes enormous energy to setting work objectives and conducting performance reviews for individual employees. Corporations go through this time-consuming and costly exercise to ensure the most favorable results for their firm. They follow this process because they know it works. Now you can benefit from this same process.

You know your personal goals and you have taken the time to create a goal log. In your action plan, you have identified the steps you have to take and you are taking action toward them. You probably also came to the realization that you need a job or a business to help you accomplish some of your dreams and desires. If not, you already have that job or business and are going to work for a reason, *your* reason.

Let's first realize that the reason we go to work is different for each of us. The main reason we go to work is to realize one of our dreams or desires. When I ask people why they go to work, most of them reply, "to earn a living" or "to make money." When I question them further I find out their true motivation. Most of us go to work to satisfy a personal need, desire or dream that we want to eventually fulfill. Work is only a stepping stone to help us get what we want out of life—it is part of the price we pay to live a dream. Why do *you* go to work? What is your underlying reason?

Once you know your motivation for going to work, you will be more motivated to go, and you will do a better job at it while you are there. Consider your job or business and what you are doing as a stepping stone to where you want to go, what you want to be or what you want to have. All of these relate to your dreams and desires.

So when you go to work, know what you expect from your job. What are the three most important things that you want from your job? If you don't know or if you can't answer this question, you are not taking control of your life or your future and you are leaving life to chance and circumstance. I am sure your organization has three important goals that they want you to accomplish while in their employ. Should you not also make *them* aware of *your* top three goals? This is part of a win/win strategy.

Your job or business has expectations of you. You should have expectations of your job or business in return. Make sure you know what these expectations are, and make sure the people you report to know them as well, and are in agreement. Then together everyone can win.

In most organizations the expectations of management for salespeople is revenue- or volume-based, while salespeople's own expectations are to have the freedom and support to do their job, and to be well rewarded or recognized for doing it. You have already reviewed and determined your personal goals; now let's take a look at the organizational goals that you are expected to meet or surpass. Do you know your revenue or volume targets? If you don't, you'd better find out what they are, because without them you have nothing to work toward.

So the first thing we do is to set that S.M.A.R.T. goal, as discussed earlier. Let's pretend your goal or target is to sell and deliver $1 million of new revenue within the fiscal year for your organization. How do you intend to meet it? Do you have a plan? That is what the goal log is all about. The goal log works for you at work as it does in your personal life. You go through each of the same steps you did earlier. However, when it comes to the action plan portion, you have a few more steps to consider.

In detailing your action plan you have to take history into consideration. What can the past tell you about seasonal trends, favorable market conditions, competitive activities, your call-to-close ratios, etc.? Knowing these and other sorts of information can benefit you considerably.

You should first review the past, as it is likely to repeat itself. Then map out your target as finely as you can by periods—quarters, months, weeks, days. You will find at the end of this section a chart titled the Sales Results Worksheet, broken down by month, which may be of assistance to you. Each of these periods becomes a sub-target or sub-goal and should be monitored and measured accordingly. But in order for you to meet these sub-goals, you have to do something. That something is your behavior.

As a salesperson you have to demonstrate appropriate behavior. You have to be constantly filling the funnel with suspects (potential customers), qualifying them to become prospects, making presentations, acquiring new business that will become customers, and following up. You also have to maintain and develop more business from existing customers, handle requests, go to meetings, complete all kinds of reports and maintain a positive and enthusiastic attitude, no matter what. There is a lot of behavior that you have to demonstrate.

You also have to know your ratios for your behaviors. For example, how many telephone calls do you have to make to get a face-to-face appointment, how many appointments turn into a presentation, how many presentations result in a sale? At the end of this section you will find a Bull's Eye Behavior Worksheet which may be of help to you.

However, if you don't know your ratios, you will first need to track your behavior, which is not all that difficult, and worth the effort in the long run. At the end of this section you will also find a Bull's Eye Tracking Worksheet. You can modify this worksheet to fit your own particular needs. Simply list the working days of the month down the left side of the page and then identify all the behaviors you engage on a daily basis. Each day track those behaviors by occasion or time. The objective is to keep track of your daily behaviors monthly to determine the time spent, and your averages, or ratios. This will in turn help you in adjusting your behaviors to achieve greater results.

Let me share an experience I once had in sales and how tracking my behaviors helped me better organize my behaviors and timing, which in turn led to more sales.

At one stage in my life I wanted to learn everything I could about franchising, so I decided to sell franchises. The franchising company would provide me with leads from advertising and from inquiries received through a toll-free 1-800 number. Each day they would send me a batch of leads to follow up on. From the very beginning I decided to track my behaviors and results so that I could measure the feasibility of doing what I was doing, as I was on a full commission structure—paid only on results.

The first thing I did was to create a simple form with each day of the month down the left-hand side. Across the top I had headings that related to what I wanted to track. Because this was promoted nationally and my work was related more to telephone work than face to face, I had headings like dials, connected, left message, call #2, fax, mailing, follow-up, trip, presentation, close.

Each day as I sat down at my desk to follow up on leads, I would have my form in front of me and I would make a mark under each heading that applied to the behavior I was conducting. At the end of the week and the end of the month I would total up my behaviors and identify ratios. After three months I concluded what my ratios were. Here is what I learned.

It took:

150 dials to get 100 contacts;

100 suspect contacts to get 5 qualified prospects;

15 qualified prospects to get 3 to take a trip to head office at their expense;

1 out of 3 to buy into the franchise.

All of this meant that I would have to make 300 contacts or 450 dials to get 1 sale. When I worked it out financially, that one sale made me $1 per dial. If I wanted to make more sales and more money, what would I have to do? Right, make more dials.

This also meant that I had to face a lot of rejection. Imagine being rejected 285 times out of 300 calls. Discouraging, isn't it? Well, I developed an idea to combat this. Knowing I could only obtain 5 potential prospects out of 100 leads, I qualified the suspects to get to a "no" quicker. Each time I hung up the phone after getting a no, I would sing "another one bites the dust, another one gone, another one gone, this is bringing me closer to my yes, YES!" and dial the next number. This little chant kept me positive and enthusiastic. However, if I hadn't tracked my behavior I would have probably given up out of constant rejection.

The other lesson that I learned, without really tracking it at first, was about the time of day that I was calling. After a while I realized that most of the prospects had jobs and had left their home phone number, not their business number. I had the office get more information when they took the initial call to determine the best time to call and where I should be calling. Based on this information, I became increasingly more productive.

Another point is important. Numerous studies reveal that 87 percent of salespeople working the telephone give up after the first attempt. By extrapolation this means that only 13 percent follow up once. Another 10 percent give up after a second call. Only about 3 percent of reps follow up more than once. Which do you think have a higher rate of success?

To get more positive responses you have to hear more no's. You hear more no's (and more positive responses) by following up every lead and every opportunity. To get more positive responses you must be tenacious on following up leads. Get the no's out of the way. Being perseverant and persistent is the key and it requires two things: a follow-up system and self-discipline.

The vast majority of reps are not effective at following up simply because they have not developed a system that makes follow-up easy and consistent. Use the tools that make you more efficient—software programs like Tele-Magic, Goldmine, Maximizer, ACT or Outlook. There are also paper-based systems like Franklin Covey or Day-Timer. It doesn't matter which system you use; just use one. Don't shove it aside as so many reps do.

When you follow up is just as important as how you follow up. Far too many reps will follow up on a letter or fax literally weeks after it has been received. The prospect never remembers it and typically gets the rep to send another letter or fax. And the cycle begins. When you send a direct mail piece, follow up two days after the anticipated receipt. If you courier something, follow up within two days. If you send a fax, follow up within one day. If you e-mail, follow up within one day. The collateral material you send should leverage your follow-up call. Timing is absolutely everything. Delaying your follow-up call dilutes the effectiveness of your support documents. If you want more positive responses make your follow-up calls sooner. By now, you should also realize that you're going to run into voice mail. It's inevitable. In fact, the odds are about 80 percent that you will encounter voice mail in a business-to-business call.

When you do leave a voice mail message, wait three days for a response. If there is no reply, call again and wait another three days. Then again, and again, if necessary. This alone puts you into an elite category of sales reps. Remember that 87 percent of reps give up after one call. This gives you an immediate competitive advantage and shows persistence without being annoying.

Use your calendar and jot down the follow-up call. If there is no answer, leave a message, grab the calendar and jot down the next follow-up call and so on. Schedule a specific time to make the follow-up calls. Don't spread them out over the day. Don't pick up the phone on a whim and dial throughout the day. Bunching the calls keeps you focused on the task. You get it done. Also, keep in mind that the time it takes to place a call and leave a voice mail message is insignificant compared with the return. Of course, the composition of your message for each and every call is equally important. That is where advance preparation, scripting, and trial and error come into play.

This process may feel awkward at first simply because it's new. Feel the discomfort and do it anyway. If you do this for a period of 21 days, it will become a habit. The key is to determine the appropriate behaviors and times in which to conduct these behaviors. You then discipline yourself to carry out those behaviors at the appropriate times on an ongoing basis.

First of all, what is the most important part of our job as salespeople? I think it is to get new business while maintaining what we have. If that is the most important part of our job, what do we need to make the difference? Appropriate behavior is important, but without prospects or customers we have nothing.

Therefore, prospects and customers are the most important component of our jobs. Because of that, we have to be constantly thinking of prospects and clients in terms of when they want to be contacted or visited, what their needs and desires are, and what we can do for them in relation to satisfying those needs and desires.

With this in mind, when is the best time for you to be contacting and spending time with prospects and customers? For those selling business to business it is mostly between 9 and 5 on business days. For others, like real estate agents or those in business-to-consumer sales, it is mostly in the evenings and weekends. We have to determine when the best time is to be in contact with our target market and focus in on those times. I like to refer to this as revenue-generating time or pay time.

Pay time is that time of day when you can be in contact with customers, because that is where your revenue is coming from. So let's define pay-time behaviors as those behaviors that lead us to the accomplishment of our goals or sales quotas. This would include networking, prospecting, telephone, follow-up, face to face presentations, customer service, and so on. Take a moment and identify the pay-time behaviors that you need to conduct on a daily basis to meet your business goals.

Now let's take a look at when these pay-time behaviors should be conducted. As a salesperson, your job is to be proactive wherever possible and reactive less frequently. You know when your customers prefer to be called on. If you are selling business to business, you know that Monday mornings and Friday afternoons are not the best of times to be calling on prospects or clients. However, other times during the week are. Your job is to identify the best times to be in contact with your target market and to carry out those pay-time behaviors during those times.

There is also the opposite side of pay-time behaviors: behaviors required that generate absolutely no revenue—no-pay-time behaviors. These are the things we have to do as salespeople—fill out call reports, write letters, send and reply to e-mail messages, complete and submit expense reports, attend sales meetings, undertake training and attend to other corporate demands. None of these will lead to generating more revenue or pay, but they have to be done.

It is these no-pay-time behaviors that you have to control. You still have to do them, but it is when you do them that will make the difference. You must never do no-pay-time activities during pay time. Do no-pay-time activities during no-pay time—when you can't be with a prospect or customer or generate any revenue. Times like before or after closing hours, holidays, weekends, etc.

Too many salespeople do not manage their time well. They use no-pay-time behaviors as excuses to avoid pay-time behaviors. Manage your behavior activity during the appropriate pay and no-pay times and you will generate more sales, revenue and goal results.

Here are some other time management tips that may be of assistance to you.

Be Action Oriented

This is where the magic begins. By having a focus, and taking those steps-to-success daily, you start to feel good about yourself and your accomplishments. You are in control of your life and your attitude. You wake up each morning thankful for another day, with that great feeling that today is going to be worthwhile, rain or shine. Why? Because you are going to do something today to bring your dream a little step closer to reality, and you are going to congratulate yourself for having done it.

It all begins by becoming action oriented. You need a "do it now" attitude. The first two letters of goal are "go." Now is the time to get going. "Do not tell the world what you can do—show it!"

Avoid procrastination. Procrastination is the process of habitually putting things off. It is tempting to make excuses . . . "I don't have the time"; "I think they said they were going to be in meetings all day, so I won't call"; "This could take forever; I'll do it when I have a spare day."

Procrastination will cause you to miss deadlines, leading to lost opportunities and income, lower productivity and wasted time. It will lower your motivation, heighten your stress and generate frustration and anger. Is this the way you want to live?

Take control of your life now! Reverse the procrastination habit by being as clever about completing things as you have been about putting them off. Don't expect to find time to achieve your goals. The only way to get time is to make time. Start by committing to a do-it-now mentality.

A do-it-now attitude makes you a self-starter—a person who can recognize a need and take appropriate action without waiting to be told. As a self-starter you will avoid the pressure, frustration and anxiety that come from having others tell you what and how to do things. You exercise your creativity in solving problems and doing work. As a result, you are more productive. You take maximum advantage of every opportunity, your sense of timing sharpening. You seldom miss something you want because of being late. Your services become more eagerly sought after.

This type of do-it-now attitude will also help you overcome your resistance to dealing with unpleasant tasks. Don't delay your gratification by delaying the unpleasant tasks. By tackling them first, you get them over with and can get on with the more pleasant things in life.

With an action-oriented, do-it-now attitude you get more out of your day. When you complete the unpleasant or hard jobs first and you act on the big tasks, little bites at a time, you'll trim your anxiety and stress load while gaining self-respect and self-confidence. After you exert this type of discipline long enough, you will establish a routine and make a new habit. Human behavior studies suggest that if you do something every day for 21 days, it will become a habit. Be consciously action oriented for the next 21 days and you will master procrastination.

Here are some action-oriented techniques to apply each day.

Determine your most productive time of the day and dedicate it to "I" time. "I" time is for you to do whatever you have to do that will bring you closer to achieving your goals. It may be as simple as visualizing the accomplishment of your goals or doing what you have to do, for you.

Manage your goals. You have already set your goals and action plans and have prioritized the actions. Take your annual goals and break them down into months, weeks and, finally, days. Do the same with each day's activities. Break the large tasks down into small, manageable pieces. Try to accomplish some of these pieces each day. Before long you will have accomplished a large task.

End each day by writing a prioritized to-do list for the next day. At the end of each week and month do the same for the next week and month. Get organized. Use a daily planner. You will be better organized if you write down everything.

Clear your mind of clutter. Solve problems while they are small. Whatever you do, do it once, to the best of your ability, and move on. Question all tasks to make sure they are worthwhile. Do the worst or hardest jobs first.

Be decisive and remove time wasters, such as interruptions, from all of your activities.

Remember to take care of yourself by exercising, watching your diet, and maintaining a balance in your life. And when evening comes and your next day's to-do list is written, celebrate. Action that gets rewarded gets repeated. Do this for 21 days and you will be transformed into an action-oriented, do-it-now person.

Be proactive. An action-oriented person is proactive. When you are proactive, you have initiative—you can see a need, figure out how to best satisfy it, determine the appropriate time to take the right action, and proceed. When you are proactive, you lead. When you lead, you take control of yourself and get the things you want out of life.

Use Visualization Techniques

Try using visualization to help yourself become action oriented. When you set your goals you pictured something that you wanted to have, be or do. Everything we have or do is preceded by an image in our mind. Visualization is seeing the end result. It is a form of mental rehearsal. Through the use of imagination, what you see is what you will get.

Your vision of your goals must be clear. There is a difference between "dreaming" about having something in the future and "visualizing" having it in the future. The power to believe makes the difference. Visualizing implies a structured and disciplined view of what you are trying to accomplish. Through visualization you picture yourself already in possession of your goal. By visualizing you look at your goal from many different viewpoints. By examining your goal from all of the viewpoints, you see the situation clearly and can act on the aspects that will result in the greatest payback.

Go put your creed into your deed.

Ralph Waldo Emerson

Make this a daily discipline. Visualize to actualize your goals. Forget all your inhibitions. See things as you want them to be, not as they are.

Take time to sit back, close your eyes, and see yourself accomplishing your goal. You are watching a movie based on the success that you have become. Focus your attention on the results. See yourself there. Feel the emotions. See the colors, the details; hear the sounds.

If you form a clear and detailed picture of your future, ways and means of getting it will be revealed to you. Keep focusing on what you want, not on how you will do it. The laws of nature will take over. The more you visualize, the more resources you will attract. Your vision will act as a magnet. It will attract people, events and circumstances to it. It is a self-fulfilling prophecy.

And when you're having a difficult moment during the day, take the time to visualize the accomplishment of your goal. It will refocus and relax you, and the issue of the moment will matter less. The major incident of today will probably be insignificant in the future. Don't trip over molehills.

Try visualizing right now. Project yourself six months into the future. Select one of your short-range goals. Now get comfortable and close your eyes. See yourself accomplishing your goal. You are now successfully there. You made it; you're living and breathing it. Use your imagination. See all the details, hear the sounds, feel the emotions, and celebrate. Visualize this for the next five minutes. Focus on the success.

I recommend that you get into the habit of doing this daily. Your enthusiastic attitude about your vision will not only keep you motivated, it will get others excited about your dream.

Control Yourself

Just as thoughts can control feelings and feelings control behavior, the reverse is also true. If you change your behavior you can change your feelings and ultimately your thoughts. *It is not just how you feel that determines how you act, it is also how you act that determines how you feel.* For example, if you pull your shoulders back, lift your head high, force yourself to smile and cheerfully greet others, you will find your mood changing.

The same process applies to self-talk. Feed your mind negative thoughts and it will produce negative actions. Feed your mind positive, confident information and your mind will react in kind. You cannot completely control the circumstances around you, but you can control what you say to yourself and how you think.

These techniques, all easy to do, are the daily steps that will lead you to success. Each success breeds success. There will be obstacles along the way, and when they get in your way, be ready for them. You must persist. Stick to it. You will get things done, and meet your objectives and goals. Keep in mind that often when we are ready to quit, success lies just around the corner. Don't ever give up on taking action. Make your dreams happen!

Goal Log – What I Expect to Achieve at Work

Creation date: _____   Last updated date: _____

Identify goal: _____

_____

Deadline/Date: _____

Outcome:

What will I see when I get there?

1. _____
2. _____
3. _____

What sounds will I hear?

1. _____
2. _____
3. _____

What will I feel?

1. _____
2. _____
3. _____

Possible obstacles / Contingency plan _____

_____

_____

_____

Skills and behaviors required _____

_____

_____

_____

_____

Identify people, groups or resources required _____

_____

_____

_____

_____

Action Plan with Dates

Action # 1 _____

Start: _____ *Finish:* _____

Action # 2 _____

Start: _____ *Finish:* _____

Action # 3 _____

Start: _____ *Finish:* _____

Action # 4 _____

Start: _____ *Finish:* _____

Action # 5 _____

Start: _____ *Finish:* _____

Action # 6 _____

Start: _____ *Finish:* _____

Action # 7 _____

Start: _____ *Finish:* _____

Action # 8 _____

Start: _____   *Finish:* _____

Action # 9 _____

Start: _____   *Finish:* _____

Action # 10 _____

Start: _____   *Finish:* _____

Action # 11 _____

Start: _____   *Finish:* _____

Action # 12 _____

Start: _____   *Finish:* _____

Methods of monitoring and measuring progress _____

_____

_____

_____

_____

Reward: What's in it for me?   _____

_____

_____

_____

_____

I have committed myself to the accomplishment of this goal by:

_____

Signature: _____   Date: _____

Sales Results Worksheet

Sales I will obtain in the next 12 months: $ _____

Sales I will obtain broken down by month:

Jan _____   Feb _____   Mar _____

Apr _____   May _____   June _____

July _____   Aug _____   Sept _____

Oct _____   Nov _____   Dec _____

This month _____

This week _____

Each day _____

Bull's Eye Behavior Worksheet

1. In order to generate $ _____
   I need to get in front of _____ prospects.

2. In order to get in front of _____ prospects,
   I need to book _____ appointments.

3. In order to book _____ appointments,
   I need to speak to _____ prospects.

4. In order to speak to _____ prospects,
   I need to initiate _____ points of contact.

5. To initiate _____ points of contact,
   I need to: _____

   _____

   _____

   _____

   _____

   _____

   _____

   _____

   _____

   _____

   _____

   _____

Bull's Eye Behavior — Tracking Worksheet

Date: _____   Name: _____

Attempts to contact:

Leads provided: _____

Cold calls:_____

Fax:_____

E-mail: _____

Dials: _____

Referrals: _____

Networking: _____

Other: _____

_____

_____

_____

Total attempts to contact:_____

Prospects contacted (#): _____   Ratio: _____

Appointments booked (#): _____   Ratio: _____

Face to face (#): _____   Ratio: _____

Sales generated (#):_____   Ratio: _____

Sales value ($): _____   Ratio: _____

The Goal Chart

Are you doing what you set out to do? If so, are you rewarding yourself for your accomplishments? If not, are you revising your plan? Knowing how you're doing will motivate you to keep going and to make the necessary adjustments along the way. You will find two charts on the following pages that will be helpful to monitor your actions and behavior.

Here's the way it works. You take the goal categories that you identified and on the Goal Chart write each category name in the column on the left. Then, beside each category, write out the goals for each time period.

Although the chart shows time periods of Year 1, 3, 5 and long term, you may use whatever time periods you prefer. I use a six-month period for my short-range goals. I use my birthday as the beginning of a new year. I use the three- and five-year columns for my medium-range goals and "long term" for my retirement and whole-life goals.

The beauty of the Goal Chart is that it summarizes all the expectations and dreams that you intend to turn into reality. Your completed Goal Chart reminds you of what is truly important in your life. It reinforces your expectations and gives you a boost in down times. It helps you in your visualization process. It is the road map to your future.

Use this chart daily and you will no longer waste time sitting in traffic or waiting on someone. You will no longer get upset about the minor incidents in your day. Why will your attitude improve? Because you are reading your Goal Chart, reviewing your goals and visualizing their accomplishment. You are projecting your mind into a time of happiness and success by visualizing goal accomplishment. It's easy, fun and rewarding. *Your thoughts of today are your reality of tomorrow.*

My Goal Chart is with me at all times. I review it regularly, add to it as I go, and update it every six months, or as need be. My Goal Chart has kept me focused on what is important to me.

Take the time now and fill in your Goal Chart. Write down your categories and goals under the appropriate time periods. Fill in what you can now, and update it regularly.

The Monthly Monitor Chart

The Monthly Monitor Chart provides you with a method to monitor your behavior and activity. Look first at "Activities." Across the top of the chart are the numbers 1 to 31. These are for each day of the month. Down the side of the chart is a list of daily activities. Check your daily progress in each activity for each goal. Fill in the chart each day. Place a check mark next to each activity that you carried out that day.

Are you doing what you set out to do? Are you really committed? The Monthly Monitor Chart will soon tell you. If you need to, adjust your goal to more chewable pieces. You may change, or add to, this list of daily activities.

Now look at "Goals" on the Monthly Monitor Chart. Here you will list your top three goals for that month. Under each goal identify three daily actions or behaviors toward the accomplishment of that goal. Review and monitor each of these every day.

The Goal Chart summarizes your short- and long-range goals, and the Monthly Monitor Chart details what you plan to do each day and month. Combined, they serve as a great tool. The charts will remind, discipline, guide, monitor and reward you. They will make you more aware of your behaviors, pointing out when you should make adjustments. They are my guide and can be yours too. Complete the charts and carry them with you at all times. Refer to them at least three times a day. Fill in the Monthly Monitor daily and revise it monthly. The effort will help you make your dreams your reality.

Goal Chart ™

GOAL CATEGORY	YEAR 1	YEAR 3	YEAR 5	LONG TERM

Overall purpose/mission: _____

THE MONTHLY MONITOR CHART ™

	1	2	3	4	5	6	7	8	9	10	11	12	13	14	15	16	17	18	19	20	21	22	23	24	25	26	27	28	29	30	31

ACTIVITIES

Goal Review
A.M.
Noon
P.M.

I recognize and praise
I visualize and use imagery
I talk positively to myself
I am an empathetic listener
I am patient and I probe

Goal #1
Actions
1.
2.
3.

Goal #2
Actions
1.
2.
3.

Goal #3
Actions
1.
2.
3.

93

Summary

What are your work expectations and personal desires, keeping in mind that work is a stepping stone to achieving your personal dreams?

Communicate your work expectations and personal desires to your manager and set win/win objectives.

Conduct *pay-time* behaviors when customers are available—prospecting, qualifying, presentations, etc.

Conduct *no-pay-time* behaviors when customers are not available—administration, e-mail, training, etc.

Develop your proactive behaviors to be less reactive.

Complete the exercises: Goal Log, Sales Results Worksheet, Behavior and Tracking Worksheets, Goal Chart, Monthly Monitor Chart.

B3 • Targeting Your Sales Effort—Prospecting for Results

The ABC's of Targeting

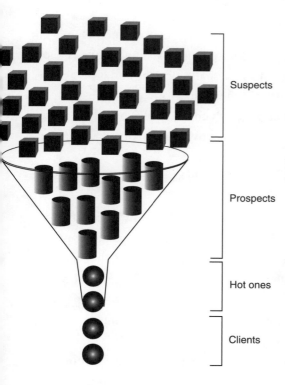

Suspects

Prospects

Hot ones

Clients

Prospecting is one of the predominant behaviors required to succeed in sales. Salespeople are required to be constantly "filling the funnel" with suspects in order for customers to come out of the spout of the funnel, thus creating new business. This new business is what keeps you, and everyone else in your organization, employed. Without new business, you will not survive, as existing business does diminish over time due to many factors—economic conditions, competition, relocation, mergers, bankruptcies, etc. New business provides continual growth in revenue, profits and market share.

For many salespeople, prospecting is the most difficult part of their job because it involves cold calls, where one faces more rejection than further down in the funnel. But cold calling has changed a lot over the years. Door-to-door visits and popping in unannounced are no longer effective means of prospecting. Prospecting has become a more sophisticated process.

Prospecting first requires some planning. Let's take a look at the prospecting funnel again and start with your target market.

Is it well defined?

Many organizations and salespeople take the traditional approach and look to the outside to define their markets. You will soon find that the opposite approach—looking inside—will prove to be more valuable to you and to your future success.

Let's define your target market from the inside out by what you already have—your customers. If you don't have any customers and you are starting up, consider who you would like to have as customers and follow the same process.

Take a look at your customer base. Identify the common elements among all customers—industry, size, location, needs, demographics, etc. There are at least three common things you will find. They all have a need for your product or service, they have the ability to pay and they have a desire—a desire to purchase from you, which is usually based on some form of personal relationship. Take the time to identify some of the other common elements and profile your customer base.

Consider these common elements and profile as criteria for your target market.

Next, identify why you are in business—what you want most from your clients—and rank them as A, B or C. If you want revenue or profit most from your clients, rank your highest revenue or profit clients as an "A," the next level as "B" and the lowest level as "C." This sort of ranking will identify the big hitters—the 20 percent that give you 80 percent of the revenue or profit. These are your most important customers—your A's. At one time they were prospects.

Let's now paint a picture of your 20 percent—your most important clients. What makes them different from the rest of your customer base, besides revenue and profit? Is it a relationship, size, need, demographics, location, market growth, competition? Identify as many elements as possible that differentiate them from the others.

Let's now refer to these differentiating elements as criteria. Once these criteria are identified, let's refer to them as Absolute (A) criteria for "A" customers, as they are also our absolute (A) customers. You absolutely need them to survive. Define the absolute criteria, based on your "A" customers, as the most important criteria that a suspect must have in order to fit into this category. These criteria must be defined clearly for your "A" customers and suspects.

Why, you ask? Knowing this will help you in identifying where you should be spending your time prospecting in order to get the best return on your investment in time—which, by the way, is limited and expensive.

Before we move on, answer the following question to yourself: Where do you spend 80 percent of your time—on the 20 percent or the 80 percent of your customer base? Where should you be spending your time? Where will you get the best return on your investment in time?

When we take a closer look at these questions we have to reconsider the traditional approach. Traditionally, salespeople have focused 80 percent of their time on the 20 percent that give them the smallest return on their time investment. In other words, salespeople are not focused where they can get the best return on time invested. They too get caught up in the crisis of the moment and take the easy route as opposed to working on a plan of return on time invested (R.O.T.I.).

The R.O.T.I. plan in prospecting is to focus your efforts where you will get the best return on your investment in time. To get that return you must know who in your target market will give you the best potential return. Profiling the top 20 percent of your existing business and focusing your efforts on those suspects with the same profile, using the pre-established "A" criteria, will give you a greater return on time invested.

"But wait a minute, Bob," you say. "If I focus all of my attention on the A's who will take care of the rest?"

Well, the answer is simple; it all depends on how you manage your time and your behavior. There are only so many A's out there—20 percent of your target market. Once you have identified them and put a plan of action together and approached them, you then move on to the next level, the B's, or those suspects that follow the profile and criteria of customers who are not absolutes, but beneficial (B) to your organization. Then there are the C's, who make up the convenient portion of your customer base. The C's are the customers, or suspects, that provide the smallest contribution to revenue or profit but are convenient to have. Using the profiles and criteria for each of the A, B and C categories will help you to identify how you should be spending your time. To give you an example, let's look at the airline industry and what makes up a profitable flight. Usually there are three classes of fares—business, economy and seat sale. As you see when you get on the plane, 20 percent of the plane is dedicated to business class and 80 percent to economy. Which fare do you think is the most profitable for the airline?

Business class is where 80 percent of the revenue comes from—20% of the customers. They are the absolute customers, as they pay for the flight. Therefore the "A" (absolute) criteria would be based on the profile of business-class travelers. That profile could include being a frequent traveler, a corporate executive or a person who enjoys and can afford the finer side of life. That profile would be used to identified the A's in the airline customer base and the suspects in the target market of air travelers.

The next level would be the economy-fare passengers. They pay less, but are greater in volume and usually fill the plane. These are the "B" (beneficial) customers. They are beneficial to the bottom line.

Then we have the seat sale fares. They fill the plane when economy fare doesn't and can be referred to as "C" (convenient) customers. They are convenient to have, but not as beneficial as full fare economy and certainly not as absolute as the business-class traveler.

The same process applies in all industries. Simply identify why you are in business and those clients who contribute the most to that focus. Identify and profile those existing (or potential) customers who contribute the most to that focus and what criteria it takes to be ranked as the most important—as an A (absolute), followed by the next level B (beneficial) and then C (convenient).

Using the same profile and criteria you used on your customer base, identify suspects in your target market using the same ranking—A, B, C. Focus your time and efforts in the same manner—mostly on the A's (60+ percent) followed by the B's (25+ percent) and then the C's (15 percent or less). If you follow this planning process for prospecting, your results will improve and your return on time invested will increase dramatically.

This is your "gain strategy." To first rank your suspects, qualify them to prospects and rank those prospects accordingly, based on your pre-identified criteria and on the information you have obtained.

Retain and Regain Strategies

There is another component to consider in the ABC's of targeting that is not related to prospecting, but deserves a mention. It is related to how you must retain and develop your A's while trying to regain past clients.

You have already identified your most important "A" customers. It is this group of buyers that contribute the most to your business focus. How much time do you spend thanking them for their business, building your relationship with them, staying close and listening to them, going the extra mile for them and contributing to their success? I think you already know what the answer is. Are you giving them the time they deserve?

You have probably heard that it is easier and cheaper to get business out of existing clients than out of suspects or prospects. This is very true and simple to do. The process is to spend the time with your A's and give them the service and attention they need and expect if you want to first retain the business you already have. Secondly, your "A" customers may need more, or something else that you offer, particularly if they are light buyers but meet your "A" criteria. This is where your highest potential for growth exists, but you have to develop the business. Thirdly, if your clients like you and the service you are giving them, they will refer you to others, or others to you. As you know, referrals are easier, more effective and more powerful than cold calls.

Take care of your customers and they will take care of you. Consider this as part of your "retain strategy," which you should take the time to consider and further develop. This is an "A" (absolute) priority.

If this has not been a priority then you have to consider past clients and develop a "regain strategy"—a strategy to gain back those clients you lost. If you and your organization do your job well in the first place, as described above, you may not need a regain strategy. However, if you do need to regain some past clients, you must ask yourself, your organization and the client why you lost them and what it will take to get them back. It is then up to you to get them back or forget them. Just remember that people only tell so many people when they are satisfied, but they tell many more when they are not. As long as it is feasible, do what you have to do to satisfy them in order to keep them and/or get them back.

On the following pages you will find some forms where you can identify your A, B and C present, past and potential clients, along with the strategies identified above. Take the time to complete them.

The ABC's of Targeting

Define **A**bsolute Criteria _____

_____

_____

Define **B**eneficial Criteria _____

_____

_____

Define **C**onvenient Criteria _____

_____

_____

Present Clients

Identify Examples of Current Heavy Buyers > **Retain**

Absolute _____

_____

Beneficial _____

_____

Convenient _____

_____

Present Clients

Identify Examples of Current Light Buyers >**Develop**

Absolute
_____

_____

Beneficial
_____

_____

Convenient
_____

_____

Past Clients

Identify Examples of Past Buyers > **Regain**

Absolute
_____

_____

Beneficial
_____

_____

Convenient
_____

_____

Potential Clients

Identify Examples of Potential Buyers > **Gain**

Absolute
_____

_____

Beneficial
_____

_____

Convenient
_____

_____

Let's now take a look at your gain strategy. You have defined your target market, using the common profile and the criteria from your customer base, and ranked each client as an A (absolute), a B (beneficial) or a C (convenient). Your next step is to identify all suspects within your target market, if you can, and rank them in the same way as well as you can.

Each organization has a different way of identifying and approaching suspects in their target market. Some organizations use a shotgun approach and go beyond target markets, while others use a more targeted approach, even on a one-to-one basis. Lead-generation methods used include direct response advertising, direct mail, telemarketing, e-mail, trade shows, public demonstrations and networking. The key is to use the methods that get you the best results in your target market, which is sometimes defined by marketing or the product development group.

If you are supplied leads, be thankful. All you now have to do, if information on them is provided, is analyze the leads. Then rank all leads as A, B or C. If no information is provided, contact the leads and either qualify them for prospect status in A,B,C priority, or reject them as no prospects. Don't try to sell them yet; just qualify them. You will learn more about how to do this in the next section on Competencies.

As you qualify suspects to prospects you have to take the information you gathered and manage a database. In a database you keep all the information you can on every prospect you come across, even after they become a client. Maintaining and updating a database is a no-pay-time activity but has all the payback rewards for being disciplined in doing it.

There are many programs on the market today that can be used for database management. Select the one that best fits your needs. Whichever program you do use, try to collect and maintain some of the information identified on the following pages.

Industry Information Form

Industry sector: _____

Size: _____

Rate of growth: _____

Trends: _____

High-tech changes: _____

New product innovations: _____

Government regulations: _____

Demographics: _____

Resources: _____

Labour: _____

Mergers/Acquisitions: _____

Other: _____

_____

_____

_____

Sources of Information:

SIC code directories: _____

Government sources: _____

Industrial guides: _____

Industry-specific directories: _____

Trade association directories: _____

Trade journals: _____

Industry experts: _____

Internet: _____

Other: _____

_____

_____

_____

Organization Information Form

Size of organization: _____

Structure of organization:_____

Rate of growth: _____

Products and services: _____

Market — local/global: _____

Geographic locations: _____

Competition:_____

Culture:_____

Mission statement: _____

Vision: _____

Objectives — short- and long-term: _____

Challenges and opportunities: _____

Needs:_____

Key contacts: _____

Decision maker(s): _____

Purchasing procedures: _____

Other: _____

_____

Sources of information:

Annual reports:_____

Association reports: _____

Government reports: _____

Internet: _____

News articles:_____

Present customers/suppliers: _____

Other: _____

_____

Client Information Form

Identify the areas you feel are valuable for you to know and to be kept current.

Creation date:_____ Last updated date: _____

Buyer Information:

Name: _____

Nickname: _____

Job title/position: _____

Company name: _____

Company address: _____

Home address: _____

Home phone: _____

Business phone/fax/e-mail: _____

Birth date:_____

Family: _____

Hobbies/recreational pursuits: _____

Physical conditions, such as back problems etc:_____

How does customer like to be contacted?

   (phone, fax, in person, letter, e-mail, etc.): _____

Preferred time of day or week for contact: _____

Secretary's name:_____

Assistant's name: _____

Other: _____

_____

_____

_____

Customer — *New*

Are there any moral or ethical issues involved in working with this customer? _____

_____

Does the customer feel any obligation to you, the company or to the competition?_____

_____

Does the sales proposal you're making require the customer to change a habit or do something unusual? _____

Is the customer overly concerned about the opinion of others? _____

What are the key problems the customer sees?_____

What are the priorities of the customer's management? Any conflicts between customer and their management? _____

Can you help with these problems? How? _____

What competitors does the customer work with? _____

How close is this relationship? _____

What suppliers to the customer do we know?_____

Other: _____

_____

If you don't want to constantly quiz the customer about themselves on details that might seem trivial to them, you could acquire information from other sources, such as their customers, suppliers, newspapers, trade publications, annual reports, receptionists, assistants and so on. In general, a detailed and well-maintained information system will prove time and again to be an invaluable tool.

Summary

Eighty percent of your business comes from 20 percent of your customers—the 80/20 rule. Prioritize your customers and prospects accordingly.

Determine the Absolute, Beneficial and Convenient criteria for each level of client and prospect.

Develop Retain, Regain and Gain strategies to maintain and increase your customer base.

Track your behaviors to determine your behavioral ratios—number of calls to appointments, appointments to qualified, qualified to close, etc.

Create a database to maintain customer information and keep it up to date at all times.

Section B • Bull's Eye Behavior—Targeting Your Sales Effort

Lessons Learned _____

_____

_____

_____

I Commit to Implement:

1. _____

_____

_____

2. _____

_____

_____

3. _____

_____

_____

I Need to Work on:

1. _____
   _____
   _____

2. _____
   _____
   _____

Section C
• • •

Bull's Eye Competencies:
Hitting, Penetrating and Staying on Target

Bull's Eye Competencies: Hitting, Penetrating and Staying on Target

Now, with a fantastic attitude and appropriate goal-driven behaviors, you need to add the "C," which stands for competencies. You need the competencies of your profession, as a lawyer or doctor needs them for theirs. You know who and where the target is; you now need to hit it and penetrate deep.

Where can you develop your competencies? Almost anywhere. As salespeople we can develop our competencies from reading books, in-class training, on the job, being coached or through trial and error. We can join professional sales associations, and in some countries, we can even become certified as sales professionals.

In this section we are going to discuss the competencies required to be a success in sales when you are face to face, having a conversation over the telephone, or communicating via e-mail with a prospect. The competencies will also be outlined in the form of a process, a step-by-step system. This process has been tried and proven internationally, in all kinds of industries, for varied goods and services.

The competencies that salespeople need are numerous, but they boil down to human interaction, communication and relationship building. Gone are the traditional days of the slick, hit-and-run "feature and benefit" dumps (overwhelming listeners with all the attractive features of the product and how it will benefit them). Why? Because every buyer has been educated by us in the past and they responded by creating their own system to maintain control over salespeople.

Traditionally, salespeople have been taught a lot of sales techniques and tactics. Most of these work for a while. However, over the years we have "trained" buyers on these techniques and tactics, as buyers see more salespeople in a day than salespeople see buyers. Buyers know that salespeople have received sales training and, when they meet with us, they usually see the same techniques and tactics being applied. As a result, salespeople have taught buyers everything they know and buyers have developed a process to counteract the actions of salespeople. The worst part is, salespeople don't even realize they have lost control, leaving the buyer in control of the interaction, when salespeople themselves should always remain in control of the sales process. It is the salesperson's responsibility to qualify the buyers. However, over the years the buyers have taken control and ended up qualifying the salespeople and their products and services.

Think about it—how do prospects respond to most of your methods and techniques? Are you in control of the process?

The time has come. Now, it is a clear-cut case of being professional and following a non-traditional proven sales results system. Do the opposite of what you may have been trained to do—that is, if you want to be different from most salespeople out there. The difference is that you will have your prospects buy from you, rather than being sold something by you. This system will help you to establish rapport and build trust, to communicate effectively and to develop and maintain lasting relationships. It is a system that will put you in control and allow you to quickly qualify prospects on several levels, to determine next steps, to prescribe solutions, to let the prospect or customer buy while retaining and developing the client relationship for more business, referrals and introductions.

Without a sales results system, salespeople are working on a hit-and-miss basis, wasting time and not getting the results they could be getting. They become slaves to the buyer's system. A professionally trained salesperson following a sales results system is a very powerful tool in any organization. Remember, without sales, there are no transactions. That translates into no revenue. Without revenue, jobs and organizations don't exist, no matter how good the product or service is.

The Buyer's System

Let's first take a look at how buyers initially react to a salesperson and why they react as they do. Then we can start to understand what the buyers have done to create their own buying system, and how they have done this.

You are a consumer or a buyer and you meet up with a salesperson, or an actual salesperson with another title that he or she is hiding behind. What is your initial reaction? Do you tell them you are so happy to see them because you have money to spend today on their particular product or service? No, I don't think so. Your first reaction may be to establish control by asking the salesperson some questions about their products or services and not answering too many of their questions. Or you may ignore them or tell them you are just looking. If this is what you are used to doing as a consumer or buyer, you are just like most consumers and professional buyers out there. Let me share a typical example with you.

Pretend for a moment that you wanted to buy an appliance or a piece of furniture for your home. You walk into a furniture store and a salesperson comes up to you and says what? Yes—"Can I help you?" This seems to be the standard line everywhere. What is your response? "No, I'm just looking." Now, why did you answer like that? You knew what you were looking for and you know the salesperson can help you.

Why do you think consumers and buyers act this way? Is it because we are bad people and we want to take advantage of salespeople? Or is it because we don't trust salespeople and salespeople need to earn that trust first? Is it also fair to say that it is okay to mislead a salesperson, because consumers know salespeople may mislead them? As a consumer you feel you are still going to get to heaven, as it is normal to lie to salespeople because you know they will lie to you.

This is the first step in the buyer's system—the buyer will initially always mislead a salesperson. It is up to the salesperson to gain the buyer's trust first.

Quite often in my training sessions I will play a game called Password with the participants—I place a word on the flip chart and ask them what words come to mind. Even with a very professional sales class I get the same answers. I get the participants to pretend they are consumers, or the general public, and have absolutely nothing to do with sales. I then place the word "salesperson" on the flip chart. What sort of words, or thoughts, come to your mind?

I hope some of those words and thoughts were positive and professional. Unfortunately, most of those words are not.

Yes, sales is regarded as the lowest form of profession there is by the general public. Yet, I believe that the profession of sales is the greatest profession of all. The world revolves around sales. Remember, without a transaction, there is no revenue and no organization can survive no matter how great its product or service is. Besides, in what other profession can you go out and get so much rejection in one day? Isn't that a great experience and a profession within itself to master! Be patient; I will share with you how to deal with rejection.

To return to the Password game—I am also getting a lot of words like "confident," "helpful," "knowledgeable," "resourceful," "professional," "courteous," "polite," etc. Now that is more like it, you say? Well, with the bad comes the good. There are many very good salespeople out there and they do set themselves apart and are very successful because of what they are doing.

Most salespeople are on time for scheduled meetings and do provide solutions within your budget and time constraints. In addition, by following the ABC, 123 Sales Results System, salespeople will learn how to quickly gain trust, eliminate surprises, uncover buying opportunities and either provide a solution within the prospect's budget and time constraints or tell the prospect "I'm sorry, I can't help you." This makes the salesperson even more professional, staying in control and still building a relationship while acquiring referrals and introductions.

One of the biggest problems in sales is that salespeople are so knowledgeable about their organization's products and/or services that they feel they have to give that information away, even if the client doesn't ask for it. I like to refer to this as free consulting. For some reason salespeople feel the more information they give the more sales they will get. Buyers like this about salespeople. It gives them a chance to stay in control. Think about it; do you freely share your knowledge with the prospect?

Let's face it, salespeople are by far the most knowledgeable people in every organization. They know the products and services well, their unique advantages and disadvantages, features and benefits, pricing, margins and discounts, production and delivery, organizational structure, competition, market and company strengths, weaknesses, threats and opportunities, mission, vision, etc. Salespeople deserve to be recognized for this, but at the same time they need to learn to be discreet, or still better, to shut up.

I provide a lot of organizations with sales and sales management consulting and coaching services. Where would my business be in three months if I were to give away everything I knew for free? I would be down the hole in no time and you will be soon too if you don't put a cap on the information you are giving away.

Why do you think prospects want to know everything you know? Right, so they can make an informed decision. But is it not also because they want to compare you to the competition? They want to know everything you know and they don't want to pay for it. I refer to this as free consulting. Think about it; what is the result of giving your expertise to the prospect?

Free consulting is the second step in the buyer's system. Buyers will use their questioning techniques to take control of the process. They will ask you tons of questions to which you normally have to hesitate before answering. You feel they are legitimate questions they are asking you and so you respond. They is nothing wrong with that, is there? Yes, there is. The person answering the questions is not in control. It is your job as a salesperson to qualify the prospect, not have the prospect qualifying you. Your job is to ask questions, not give information away, particularly for free.

The funny part is that most salespeople have not learned this yet. They give away tons of information, and then what sort of an answer do they get most of the time from the prospect? "Thank you, I want to buy"? No, I don't think so. How about, "thank you for all of the information; let me get back to you" or "I need to think it over; I'll get back to you" or "I will discuss it with the others and get back to you."

You have heard all of these lines before, haven't you? What happens? What do they really mean without saying it? Is it fair to say the prospect is misleading us again? This is step three in the buyer's system. They really mean to say "no, I am not interested" but they don't want to hurt your feelings, or figure they could never get rid of you if they did say no because you have been trained to only go for a yes. Don't worry; I will teach you the opposite—how to go for a no.

Now the prospect has misled us, gathered all the information they need for free and misleads us again. As a salesperson you end up with the impression that you have a sale coming. However, it is really only a "hope-a"—I hope I got a sale.

Because you have been well trained, you have gotten all of the prospect's contact information and you decide to follow up with them. What usually happens? Do they take your call? Do they return your voice or e-mail messages? If so, great! You have managed to gain some trust and started to develop a relationship. If not, you have fallen into the buyer's system once again. The fourth step of the system is they hide—they don't return your calls or e-mail messages. Why? Maybe because they found a better deal, a better product or service, or maybe a better salesperson—one who asked questions, took the time to show he or she cared by listening to the prospect's needs while helping the customer buy. You can tell and sell, or you can do the opposite—ask and let them buy. Keep doing what you have always done and you will get what you have always gotten.

The following pages will reveal the opposite approach to you, which will allow you to gain and stay in control so that you can qualify the prospect first, before providing any solutions or free consulting.

Summary

The "Buyer's System":

The salesperson is misled—"No need, just looking."

People will try to get as much information from the salesperson as possible—free consulting—so they can shop and compare price.

The salesperson will be misled again—"Let me think it over" or "I'll get back to you."

When you follow up with the prospect they hide—they don't return phone calls or e-mail messages.

C1 • Building Relationships

Think about a present relationship you have with a client, a partner, a spouse or a friend. How did you get it started? Try to remember your first encounter and what happened that started that relationship. Next, think about what you did to keep that relationship going.

Did either of them have anything to do with discovering commonalities, showing you cared?

In this section we are going to discover how to build and maintain long-term relationships. Relationships between people like you and me. You must first understand that people buy from people, particularly people they trust and like—people who remind them of themselves. Therefore, it is important for you to be aware of and to understand the person with whom you are building a relationship.

You will learn how to build rapport quickly so that you can gain the trust that is needed to ask questions and get answers. You will also learn about two basic communication skills—the skills of asking questions and listening to the responses. What is the point of asking questions if you are too busy thinking up other questions to ask, and not listening? You will also learn how to identify a person's dominant sense so that you can better relate to them in the way they see, feel or hear.

At one time we were taught to follow the golden rule: "Do unto others as you would have them do unto you." That was a great rule to follow. It is right to say that, to yourself, you are the most important person in the world and under the golden rule, how your treat yourself is how you should also treat others.

However, over the years the golden rule has been replaced with the platinum rule: "Do unto others as they would like to have done unto themselves." The platinum rule takes a different approach. What it is saying is that when you are with another person, treat them the way they would like to be treated, not the way you would want to be treated. Therefore, we have had to change our approach.

As a salesperson, when we meet with a prospect or a client, who is the most important person in the world? I hope you said the opposite of the golden rule and said the prospect or client. If so, great, because without a prospect or a client, you have absolutely no chance of selling anything. Do you agree? I hope so.

So, if the prospect or client is the most important person in the world when selling and we are to follow the platinum rule, we had better treat them the way they want to be treated. That means we have to be on our toes and look for all kinds of clues—clues that I will share with you shortly. But first let's look at the way we approach prospects and then understand the universal needs of buyers.

First of all, would you agree that it is a privilege to be invited to a prospect's office? Good, I certainly agree with you that it is a great privilege. But take note of the words I used in my question. Do you use the word "invite" or do you make appointments with prospects? Simply changing a few words in our language can change the scenario.

Let's go back to the initial telephone call, if that is how you get invited to a prospect's place of business. First of all, let's understand that a telephone call is an intrusion and we must approach it as such. When you make the call, do you quickly introduce yourself, state your unique benefit statement and ask if this is a good time to talk before proceeding? If the answer is yes, do you also ask permission to ask questions? If you do, you are on the right track. If not, start asking if it is a good time to talk and seek permission to ask questions. If it is not a good time, ask what a good time would be to call back, and call back then.

Within the first three minutes you should be able to identify whether the prospect is qualified to meet or not by asking a few simple pre-planned questions. If they are qualified, rather than saying "I would like to meet with you and show you how we can satisfy your need, or provide a solution to your problem," try saying something like "Do you ever invite people like myself to your office to discuss these problems, and possible solutions, in greater detail?" You will get a yes most of the time, and by asking to be invited you are setting a different tone for the meeting. Then, of course, when you arrive at the meeting you thank them for inviting you.

Now you are at the meeting. What did you bring with you? Did you bring a bag full of information, a brochure, some samples, etc.? I hope not, because if you did, you will automatically lose control. The prospect will want to see what you have in the bag and you will want to show them everything you have in it.

The secret of a first call is to go in with nothing more that a notepad and a pen or pencil. This initial phase is to build trust and to make the prospect feel important and comfortable with you.

Now let's take a look at the universal needs of buyers.

There are basically four universal needs that we must address to satisfy buyers. The first one is that buyers need to be understood. That means we must listen to them and question them to better understand them. The problem many salespeople have is that they don't listen and, worse yet, they don't question the answers they receive to get even more information. There will be more on this in the questioning section.

The second universal need is that buyers need to feel welcomed. How do you welcome people who come and visit you at home? Do you welcome prospects and clients the same way, even in their own premises?

Buyers have the need to feel important. How important do you make them feel in your presence? Asking questions and taking notes is one way to do that.

Finally, they also have the need to feel comfortable. How can you make them more comfortable? The following sections will help you with all of these needs

Building a long-term relationship

The Relationship Selling Model

An Investment	
1. Time	4. Money
2. Energy	5. Status (reputation)
3. Ability	

+

Genuine Sincere Assistance

+

Trust

=

Relationship
A commitment from both parties

C1.1 • Building Rapport

rap.port (from the Old French "to bring back")
1. relationship. . . 2. agreement. . . 3. harmony

Webster's Dictionary

In order to build a relationship, you must consider a number of factors—the first must be to establish trust. Trust can be established in a number of ways, but the quickest way is through building rapport. Once rapport is established and the prospect trusts you, you can proceed to ask questions and get information. Without trust, the prospect will not answer any questions. This is the most important first step in the selling process you are about to learn.

In contemporary use, "building rapport" refers to achieving a sense of relationship, agreement and harmony. However, the word "rapport" actually derives from Old French and means "to bring back." In sales, the concept of "bringing back" is key to what is meant by "building rapport."

Building rapport is an ongoing process that is *only beginning* early in the sales effort. Therefore, you will have both *short-range* and *longer-range* objectives for building rapport.

Objectives

These are some typical *short-range* objectives for building rapport:
• Make the prospect comfortable in the sales situation
• Begin to find out why the prospect is there — gain a sense of the prospect's need and how you can learn more about that need
• Ensure that you will be able to continue the sales effort beyond its opening moments.

Objectives such as these must be met if you expect the prospect to be around long enough for you to earn the right to proceed.

Here are some typical *longer-range* objectives for building rapport:

- Gain attention so that you are able to begin a dialogue with the prospect
- Begin building a foundation of rapport between yourself and the prospect—the sense of "harmony, affinity and agreement" that is key to your success
- Earn the right to proceed—ensuring that the prospect will stay with you (and return if necessary), thus positioning yourself to learn about the prospect's need and complete the sale.

The Rapport Pie was developed through the study of neurolinguistic programming (NLP) by Drs. Bandler and Grinder. "Neuro" (from the Greek "neuron"—nerve) denotes your nervous system, which makes you feel well when your body is in harmony and "out of sync" when you feel ill. "Linguistic" (from the Latin "lingua") denotes the way you communicate. Programming is the system or organizational pattern needed to achieve a desired result.

NLP is literally the science of how to most effectively communicate with your brain and nervous system to produce various behavioral results. The most important skill for a salesperson is the ability to communicate. Through the use of NLP strategies you will learn how to be a better communicator, view a situation from the other person's point of view and build rapport in a short period of time.

The Rapport Pie

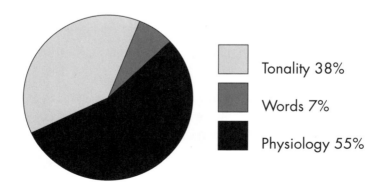

Tonality 38%

Words 7%

Physiology 55%

You will note that the most important piece of the rapport pie (55 percent) is physiology—your physical body. What it means is that your physical body has more to do with building rapport than the tone of your voice or the words that you use. Physiology can be used, and is very important, in face-to-face situations.

Tonality, at 38 percent, ranks second in building rapport. Tonality is the tone of our voice—high to low. It is also the rate of our speech—slow to fast. Tonality is most important when working on the phone.

Words represent the smallest portion of the rapport pie, at 7 percent. Yet how much emphasis have we placed on words alone in the past? The words you used may have done you more harm than good.

So where should we be focusing our efforts to quickly build rapport? Not on words, but on physiology. And the way to do that is through matching and mirroring. Matching and mirroring is simply taking notice of the prospect's body language, tonality and words, and mirroring, matching or reflecting them back to the prospect.

Earlier I mentioned that people buy from people, particularly people they trust and like—people who remind them of themselves. When you match and mirror, the prospect sees himself or herself in you, making them more comfortable with you. However, you must also understand that matching and mirroring does differ from mimicking. Mimicking is doing as they do *when* they do it. That is not what we are talking about. You take notice of the way the person opposite you sits, stands, walks, talks and the words they use. You simply match and mirror them over time, not at the exact same time. Many salespeople do this naturally and don't even know they are doing it. They make prospects very comfortable first by matching and mirroring and then move on to the next step of the sales cycle. But we are not there yet. Let's take some time to understand all three components of the rapport pie.

Physiology is the biggest contributor to building rapport and there are many ways to match and mirror physiology. When you first meet someone, what is the first thing that you do with them, physically? You usually walk up to them and shake their hands, I hope. When we shake hands with someone, we have always been told to have a firm grip. Now pretend for a moment that the person you are meeting has a very soft handshake and you give them a firm grip. Do you think you make them feel comfortable and important or overpowered and intimidated? The latter. What is important in this first step is to let them squeeze your hand first and within a second match that same squeeze back.

I use this technique all the time, especially when I speak before large audiences. I will greet people at the door as they come in. They don't even know who I am most of the time and I am just standing there greeting them and shaking their hands. The funny thing is I am matching all of their handshakes and starting to build rapport with them. When I get introduced and appear on stage, they are saying to themselves, "Hey, I know him, he was the guy at the door; he is just like me." Why? Because I made them feel comfortable with me by matching their handshake.

There are many other physical acts that can be matched and mirrored. You can walk at the same pace as the other person, stand like they do, sit, lean, point or match their hand and facial gestures. The most important part is that they see themselves in you, without your mimicking them. So be aware of the other person's physiology, and over time, mirror and match.

Tonality can be matched by speaking at the same rate and the same pitch. This technique is similar to the handshake. How do you think a soft slow-speaking person will feel with someone who is a loud fast talker? Do you think the prospect is feeling comfortable?

When doing telephone work, tonality is your greatest asset because it is the person at the other end who answers the phone and speaks first. You have to clue in and match their tone and pace. Mind you, although they can't see your physiology, you should still be standing tall and speaking up. Too many salespeople lean on their arm on the desk, holding the phone and speaking down. They sound depressed. Try standing up and looking at yourself in a mirror on the ceiling and you will notice how much better your voice sounds. You will find that it is clearer, more confident and more enthusiastic.

Although words play a small part in building rapport, they are still important to match and mirror. All you have to do is listen to the words they are using and use them yourself. Listen for and use their buzz words and their terminology. For example, if they refer to a hotel as a resort, use the word resort. If they say "correct" or "right" a lot, use the word "correct" or "right" with them when you are speaking.

Now, how are you going to remember the prospect's physiology, tonality and words? What do you have with you on your first call? Right, only a notebook and a pen or pencil. Use them (in this case, after your meeting) to help remember these things.

Dominant Senses

Now let's move on to another component of understanding people—determining their dominant sense. As you know, we have five dominant senses—sight, sound, touch, smell and taste. Research has proven that the three dominant senses of the five are sight (visual), sound (auditory) and touch (kinesthetic) and that each of us possesses one of these senses as a dominant sense and one as a secondary sense.

When we take the time to understand and determine the dominant sense of the person we are in contact with, we can change our language and presentation style to improve communications. By using visual words and visuals we can better relate with visual people. The same applies to those whose dominant sense is auditory and to those who are kinesthetic. First let's take a look at people who are dominantly visual.

Visual people see the world. Everything is sight-based. Even when they speak they see a picture in the mind's eye and speak to the picture. Because of this, visual people usually speak fast; they often don't finish their sentences because they are on to the next picture in their mind. Visual people also have a good visual memory and are good with directions.

It is very important for us to listen to the type of words the other person is using. Visual people will use visual phrases, like "picture this," "show me how it works" or "see what I mean."

To appeal to and communicate effectively with a visual person, you must show them your product or service using visual words and, of course, visuals—pictures, PowerPoint and/or flip chart presentations. Remember, they have a need to *see* the way things are.

Unlike visual people who *see* the world, auditory people *hear* the world. To an auditory person the words used are the most important.

Auditory people use phrases like "hear this," "tell me how it works," "do you hear what I am saying?" Auditory people will structure the sentence in their mind, repeat it to themselves a few times and then speak it slowly and accurately. Why? Simply because words are so important to them, as are sounds.

To appeal to and to communicate effectively with an auditory person, you must tell them about your product or service using auditory words and, of course, documentation—specifications, warranties, procedures, etc. Remember, they have a need to hear or read the way things are, not see the way things are.

Unlike visual and auditory people who see and hear the world, kinesthetic people *feel* the world. To a kinesthetic person touch and feelings are the most important. Kinesthetic people use phrases like "it feels good," "I sense how it works," "do you know what I am saying?" Kinesthetic people will feel hot or cold about you. Why? Simply because feelings, or gut instinct, are so important to them, as is touch.

To appeal to, and to communicate effectively with a kinesthetic person, you must appeal more to their emotions about your product or service using kinesthetic words and, of course, samples they can touch and feel. Remember, they have a need to touch and feel the way things are, not see or hear the way things are.

You now need to take some time to decide what *your* dominant sense is, and your secondary sense. There are exercises available to help you determine your dominant sense. Once you know your dominant and your secondary sense you will note that it is a lot easier to communicate with a person who has the same dominant senses, and more challenging with those whose dominant sense you do not have.

For example, I am a visual-kinesthetic type of person. It is easy for me to understand and quickly bond with other visual and kinesthetic types of people. However, my challenge is more with auditory people. As a visual I speak quickly and as a kinesthetic, I speak from the heart and reveal my feelings. When communicating with an auditory person, I have to learn to slow down and fully enunciate my words. Also, because words are important to auditory people I have to make sure that I don't make any spelling mistakes and that I speak more slowly than I do with visual people. The other challenge is for me not to complete their sentences, as I see too many visual (sales) people doing this. Not only is it rude, it is creating communication barriers, destroying potential relationships and killing a potential sale.

In order to communicate effectively and to build relationships, we have to learn to communicate in all three senses, in a manner that is consistent with the other person's dominant sense. It is not always easy, but if you take the time to listen, you will find that it does become easier.

Understanding the other person's dominant sense will come in very handy toward the end of the sales process when you are making your presentation. However, it is better to mention it here so that you can start listening for clues now! [There are excellent materials available on Neuro-Linguistic Programming (NLP) that go into much greater detail on visual, auditory and kinesthetic characteristics, related eye movements, and so on.]

Besides senses, there are other areas you should be observing. There are many hints you can get from physical surroundings, mannerisms, physical appearance and characteristic traits. They are all worth taking note of, in your notebook, after you leave. But there is a word of caution: don't make any assumptions. A messy desk does not always mean that the person is disorganized. However, it *would* tell me to not just leave a brochure but to review it with him or her first.

Summary

Ask if it is a good time to talk; if not, reschedule the call.

Ask permission to ask questions and/or take notes.

When setting appointments, ask to be *invited*.

Adopt the relationship selling model.

Use the components of the Rapport Pie—physiology 55%, tonality 38%, words 7%—to build rapport.

Match and mirror, don't mimic, people with whom you want to build rapport.

Identify the other person's dominant senses—visual, auditory, kinesthetic.

Observe and take note of the physical surroundings/appearance, mannerisms, traits.

C.1.2 • Asking Questions

Questioning and listening are the most important communication skills required in this sales process, and they contribute directly to building relationships once rapport has been established. In this chapter and the next one, you will learn some questioning and listening skills. Once we have mastered these questioning and listening skills we can go on to the next steps in the ABC, 123 Sales Results System.

When starting the sales process you need to build rapport and then ask questions. The best way to start is with an open-ended question so that the prospect starts talking. If you have not first built rapport with the prospect, they will not answer your questions honestly. So make sure you have first established rapport. You can always tell when you have established rapport just by noticing how much the prospect starts to open up to you. It is as if they will never stop talking. Of course that is your job, to establish rapport, to get the prospect talking, keep them talking and direct them with questions that will lead them to where you want to go, while you gather more information and facts. But first, where is it that you want to go; what is your objective? You need to answer this question before you proceed.

The first objective of the ABC, 123 Sales Results System is to establish rapport. The next one is to set up the parameters of how you are going to proceed so there are no surprises for either party. The third objective is to determine whether the prospect is qualified, so you need to ask questions that will uncover the problems that you have solutions for, whether there is a budget to solve those problems, and when and how a decision would be made. If there are no problems, there are no needs to provide solutions for. If there is no money, how can you proceed? If they can't make a decision sooner or later, how can you proceed with getting them to buy? You must first meet these objectives by asking questions and staying in control of the sales process.

It is only after you have gathered all of this information that you can summarize and determine whether the prospect is qualified and whether there is an opportunity to do business or not. If not, you abort and move on to the next prospect, rather than having the prospect qualifying you and telling you "let me think it over and get back to you." If there is an opportunity to do business, your next objective would be to prescribe a solution and present it to the prospect.

You now realize how important it is to stay in control of the process. The ABC, 123 Sales Results System requires you to meet your first three objectives before you can summarize and determine whether there is an opportunity to do business, and make a presentation providing a solution, or not. In the buyer's system, you provide that information in the second step.

Salespeople need to understand that there is no reason for doing a presentation if there is no need, money or decision-making capability. Therefore, it is your job to qualify, close/abort or continue, if qualified, present, and then maintain and develop the account for more business and referrals.

Everything discussed above is communications based. I am sure you will agree that if we do not communicate effectively, we will not make a sale. We have already discussed how we can improve our communications by identifying and mirroring the dominant sense of the person to whom we are speaking. However, communication is a two-way process involving both parties. The process that you need to master is that of asking questions, questioning the answers and staying in control. If this is not the process you have been following the change will be difficult at first, but with trial and error and continuous practice and application, you will soon master these important communication skills.

First let's understand why people buy. People buy because they want to satisfy a need. However, many people think that the process of buying is intellectual and requires the salesperson to provide features and benefits. Well, folks, once again, the opposite is true. People don't buy for intellectual reasons; they buy for emotional reasons. They justify their purchase intellectually. And yes, there is a role for features and benefits, but it comes later in the process.

In order to be successful in our communications we must first understand our prospects. We do this by asking questions and listening. Only in this way can we qualify our prospects and determine if there is a need, and if we can provide a solution to that need. Only after this point can we communicate our position.

Let's first understand why you ask questions. By asking questions you learn a lot, you uncover needs, you make the other person feel important and that contributes to building a lasting relationship. There are millions of reasons for asking questions, but there is one reason that is most important for salespeople to understand, and to master.

It is the salesperson's responsibility to qualify prospects, yet it is the prospect who qualifies the salesperson most of the time. This is witnessed by the prospect asking questions of the salesperson and the salesperson answering those questions and giving free consulting. It is the salesperson's responsibility to gather information, not give it away. It is when salespeople start to give information away—free consulting—that they start to lose control.

The main reason for salespeople to ask questions is to maintain control of the sales process—to build rapport and to gather information to determine whether the prospect is qualified for the solutions you provide and then to make a decision to proceed or to abort. When a salesperson is not in control of the process they have fallen into the buyer's system.

So how do you get information and stay in control of the sales process? Ask questions. It is always the person who is asking the questions that is in complete control. The person who is answering the questions thinks they are in control, but in reality they are not. It is the salesperson's responsibility to be in control of the process, but it is the client who should think he or she is in control.

Let's pretend (a technique you will learn about later) you are interviewing someone for a job in which they will be reporting to you. You start off the interview by getting the interviewee comfortable and start asking questions of the individual you are considering. You are in control of the process at this point. The interviewee answers all of your questions and thinks they are in control because they are giving good accurate answers—they are in reality selling themselves. You are impressed, as they answered all of your questions, and you end the interview by telling him/her that you will get back to them. Why? Because you have other candidates to consider and want to make the right selection. Notice the similarity to the buyer's system—you the interviewer, the buyer, was in control.

Your next interview starts off in the same way, with a little small talk to get the candidate comfortable, but the difference here is the candidate starts off by asking you questions. Rather than answering questions, they are asking questions of you and qualifying the opportunity. You in turn start answering their questions. You think you are in control, but in reality the interviewee is. The interview ends with the interviewee asking you what the next step is, as opposed to you telling them.

Now it is decision time. Which of the above two candidates would you hire, the two having equal qualifications, but taking a different approach? The one who sold themselves and answered all of your questions, or the one who showed interest and asked a lot of questions? Let's understand why the second candidate would win out. By asking questions the candidate was showing they were interested. By listening to your responses, they made you feel important, while demonstrating their communication skills and desire to learn. The interviewer made the candidate feel important in the first interview by listening to their answers, but the candidate did not demonstrate those important questioning and listening skills, or a desire to learn. They were only interested in themselves and trying to sell themselves accordingly.

Think about the way you have been approaching prospects. Are you like the first candidate in the interview or the second one? Which one would you like to be?

The difference is in the approach you take. If you truly believe that the prospect is the most important person in a sales interaction, then you will have no problem following this system. However, if you think that you or the products or services that you represent come first, then I wish you all the luck in the world. Because sales is not about you or your products or services, it is about the other person, their problems and their needs, and that must always come first.

We ask questions to stay in control of the process and to keep the prospect talking, so we can determine if there is a need that we can satisfy, while we contribute to building a long-term relationship. The secret behind asking questions is also to have prospects buy from you. Think about it. Do you prefer to be sold something or do you prefer to buy something? Questions contribute to a self-discovery process, which is also a buying process. The salesperson asks the prospect questions that lead the prospect to discover their own needs and solutions within their budget and decision-making process. They must come up with the answers themselves—you can't tell them, as they must own those answers. You just have to know what questions need to be asked in order to get the answers you are seeking.

So what are the questions that you need to ask to stay in control and to get the answers you are seeking? First, let's get an understanding of the types of questions that can be used in the process and why they are used. Then we will take a look at the questions that can be asked.

Open-ended Questions

Typically open-ended questions begin with what, how, who, why and where.

Purposes

- To allow people to feel a greater sense of participation in an interview
- To give the discussion a more conversational tone
- To encourage prospect to respond at length, providing you with information critical to the sale
- Not only useful as fact-finding, but to uncover underlying attitudes, opinions and feelings
- To help prospects clarify their thinking
- To help prospects to identify and verbalize their own needs
- To provide you with information in order that you may paraphrase them

Examples

How does this affect your business?

What is it you like about brand X?

Why is that important to you?

Why do you say that?

Take the time to generate open-ended questions that will be useful in your sales interview, starting with the first question that you would use when you first meet up with a prospect.

Directing Questions

Occasionally, you need to point your customer in a particular direction—a direction that will provide new information in areas of specific interest to you.

Purposes
- To stimulate thinking in new directions.
- To cause the customer to evaluate the consequences of not acting.
- To force a reply that you wish to hear.
- To force a choice in order to help you guide the discussion in the right direction.

Examples
What would happen if . . . ?
What would happen if you didn't . . . ?
So you think it would be wise to . . . ?
Do you prefer . . . ?

Questions that perform these functions for you are also referred to as leading questions. Note that leading questions can either open up the discussion or focus in the discussion, depending on your purpose at a specific point in time.

Questions that fulfill the first two purposes open up discussion.

Questions that fulfill the last two purposes focus in discussion.

Take the time to generate directing questions that will be useful in your sales interview.

Fact-Finding and Closed-Ended Questions

When you need short, to-the-point answers.

Purposes
- To gather facts
- To "break the ice" and set the "ground rules"

- To attract the attention of someone unwilling to talk or to re-focus the conversation
- To check for degree of understanding or interest
- To confirm an agreement

Examples of yes or no closed-ended questions
1. Would this plan meet your needs?
2. Do you currently buy from more than one supplier?

Examples of fact-finding closed-ended questions
1. How many people do you employ?
2. What brand of product are you currently using?

Take the time to generate fact-finding and closed-ended questions that will be useful in your sales interview.

Be prepared when you contact or meet a prospect. Create a list of questions that will uncover potential problems that you have solutions for. Start by listing all the potential problems you have solutions for. Then develop some questions that will help uncover some of those problems. In the next chapter, on qualifying prospects, we will discuss how you need to identify three to five problems by asking a lot of questions. The more problems identified, the higher the likelihood of making a sale.

As you proceed to ask questions, you can also expect the prospect to be asking you questions, and this is where you can lose control. You lose control by answering the questions, and even more if you get into a lot of details. Your job is to introduce yourself, and state your name and company and your unique benefit statement on how you help organizations like theirs in this specific industry. But before you can tell them anything, you need to know a lot about them. How you do this will be discussed in greater detail in the next section under "Setting the Parameters." For now, let me just share with you how to maintain control.

When asked a question, you need not respond, as you may have always done. When you are asked a question, first take the time to respect the question. That is done by giving the prospect a compliment—something along the lines of "that is a great question, John." Then you need to repeat the question and reverse it, or turn it back to the prospect—i.e., "Would that be important to you, and why?" By doing this you obtain additional information and clarity and stay in control.

Reversing helps you in several ways. It keeps the prospect talking, allowing you to gather more information, which leads to more questions. Reversing also shifts the focus from you to the prospect, where it belongs. Questions show you are interested in the prospect; they build rapport and support your credibility.

Another way of staying in control when asked a question is to again respect the question by complimenting the prospect and providing a brief answer, but to end with a question back to the prospect. If you don't, you are giving the prospect another chance to question you and you will eventually lose control and end up in the buyer's system.

A word of caution when you are being asked the same question twice—answer it; don't antagonize the prospect. Ask another question and move on. It is rare that a prospect will ask the same question twice.

Questions can also be used to handle objections. When the prospect presents an objection to you, respect it and reverse it, turning it back to them. Quite often I will get the objection that I am too expensive. I always say, "That is an interesting observation; why do you think I am so expensive?" I always get an answer as to why I am and—you know what?—their answer doesn't really matter to me, so long as it is their answer and not mine. You should never have to justify your prices or fees, your product, your service organization or what you do for a living. Make it a practice to stop justifying and start reversing the pressure to where it belongs—back to the prospect.

It is very important for you to keep the prospect talking. If they are not talking, you end up talking, and that is dangerous. The 80/20 rule applies here, as it does elsewhere. You job is to get the prospect talking so that you are listening 80 percent of the time. The other 20 percent of the time you should be asking questions.

The best way to keep the prospect talking is by asking questions and by questioning their answers. As you hear certain concerns in their answers, you direct the prospect to where you want to go. You then ask fact-finding questions and determine the bottom-line problems, the costs associated with those problems, and how it affects the organization and the individual you are speaking with. It is when you have answers to all of these questions that you stop the line of questioning and move on to questions that will uncover other potential problems.

Some techniques you can use to keep the prospect talking are using simple statements like, "That's interesting; tell me more." This is particularly useful when the prospect is showing interest in your product or service. Rather than going for a close, get them to tell you why they are interested or what it is that made them feel as they do. Let them sell themselves.

You can also use your body language and facial expressions to show that you are actively listening and you want to learn more—use eye contact, nod, react, etc. If you are a woman, you probably already know how to use body language. If you are a man and you're not sure how to use your body language, just watch two women talking to each other. You will witness listening skills and probing body language like you have never seen before.

Another point to remember is to always question the answers three to five levels deep to get more clarity and information. Don't ever just accept the first answer to a question. For example, let me ask you a question: "Why do you go to work?" You probably answered, to make money. Now question the answer—"make money to do what?" Question the answer, question the answer, and you will soon discover why you really go to work. You will realize that you go to work for your personal reasons—by working you are taking steps toward the realization of a personal dream. Realize that and you will be more motivated in going to work.

Another technique to get and keep the prospect talking is the "let's pretend" or magic wand technique. The let's pretend technique is simply asking in a way that leads to a response. For example, "Let's pretend that nothing was impossible and that you could have a solution to that problem; what sort of a solution do you feel would work best?" Or, "If you had a magic wand, what would be the ideal solution you would wish for?"

When communicating with a prospect you will sometimes get wishy-washy answers from them. If you are not sure what they mean, question them. You will always get improved clarity by asking additional questions. Quite often I hear answers like "maybe," "leave it with me," or "I'll think if over and get back to you." I always question these answers because they are not clear to me. For example, "When you say maybe, what does that mean?" or "When you say you will think it over and get back to me, what exactly will you be thinking over and when can I expect to hear back from you?" If I don't have clear answers, I have nothing but a hope of a sale. I always make it a point to get a clear response so I know exactly where I stand.

By asking questions, you will remain in control. Questions will help you gain a lot more information. Questions will handle objections and concerns. Questions show that you care and that you are interested and willing to learn more. Questions help in self-discovery and it is the self-discovery process that gets people to buy, because they own the answers. Master the act of questioning and staying in control of the sales process. But make sure you listen to what the answers are, and question the answers.

Summary

Ask questions that will help you gather the types of information you need.

Use *open-ended* questions when you want people to open up and talk.

Use *directing* questions when you need a specific answer or need to move the conversation in a specific direction.

Use *fact-finding* questions to gather the information you need.

Use *closed-ended* questions when you need to focus the conversation, reach conclusions, etc.

Use a deliberate sequence of questioning that will take you and your customer where you need to go. Start by first identifying the problems that you have solutions for. Then create a list of questions you need to ask that will help you uncover whether there are any problems that you have solutions for.

Determine what information you need.

Use a mix of open, directing, fact-finding and closed questions that will gather that information for you and keep the discussion on track.

Use the "let's pretend" or magic wand technique to get them talking about their ultimate desires as if nothing were impossible.

Constantly evaluate whether you are getting the information you need and, if not, adjust your line of questioning accordingly.

Don't assume that a customer will always "open up" with open questions, "focus in" with closed questions, etc. Be ready to rephrase questions or adjust your approach if you are not getting the answers you need, or if you are not moving the discussion in the direction it needs to go.

Stay in control. When asked a question, respond with a compliment— "That is a good question, John"—repeat and reverse the question, turning it back to the prospect—"Would that be something important for you to consider, and why?" They will almost always elaborate on the question asked and give you more information. When asked the same question twice, provide a brief answer.

Be sure that you don't give your customer the impression that he or she is being "grilled."

When asked a question about price or a solution early in the cycle, mention that you will give them an answer to that question soon but you need to gather more information first—"you are on page 10 and I am only on page 4."

When you get answers like maybe, leave it with me, or any statement that is unclear, question it by asking what they mean. You need to be sure you fully understand where they are at.

If they are showing interest in your product or service, ask them what it is that makes them feel that way. It will give the prospect a chance to sell himself more.

Listen to the answers to your questions.

Listen 80 percent of the time. Ask questions for the other 20 percent of the time.

Focus on what the customer is saying. Don't be thinking about your next question.

Avoid formulating your next question while the customer is talking—particularly if that sort of activity easily distracts you from listening.

Always question the answers for more detail. It is when you question the answer three or four levels down that you can get to the root of the problem.

C1.3 • Listening

In the last chapter you learned that by asking questions you remain in control. Questions help you gain a lot more information. Questions handle objections and concerns, and questions show that you care and you are interested and willing to learn more. Questions also help in self-discovery and it is the self-discovery process that gets people to buy. But there is no point in asking questions if you are not prepared to listen effectively.

You may find it difficult to listen effectively. If you are one of those people who are constantly thinking of what to ask next and not listening to the answers you are getting, you need to change quickly. I used to be one of those people and I changed.

First I scripted the questions that I needed answers to and placed them in some order on a page in my notebook—a page I could refer back to when I needed to. That in itself took some pressure off me. Then I applied the "question the answer" technique discussed in the chapter on asking questions. Then, rather than having to think up the next question, I would listen to what the prospect was saying and I would question their answer. By scripting my questions in advance and questioning the answers I became a more effective listener. I not only learned a lot more by getting more information, I earned a lot more respect, resulting in long-term relationships.

The other thing that I did to help me become a more effective listener was to monitor myself daily using the Monthly Monitor Chart. I monitored myself on two things—"I am patient and I probe" and "I am an empathetic listener." I would review these points daily and I would check myself daily on my effectiveness in these areas. As a matter of fact, they are still on my monthly monitor because I realize how important they are in sales and I don't ever want to lose sight of them. You may want to consider doing the same, because being patient and probing and listening empathetically are extremely important areas to master in this sales process.

Just in case you don't know what I mean by being an empathetic listener, let me explain. People are usually sympathetic—they feel sorry about something that may have happened such as the loss of a loved one. Sympathy means you feel what your prospect feels. If you feel that your price is too high or that your terms are unreasonable, just like the client, then you have crossed the line. Sympathy (in sales) is bad. Sympathy means you are no longer capable of working out an effective solution, or more typically, of attempting to sell value.

However, to be empathetic is quite different. To demonstrate empathy is tough at first, but once mastered, it will make the biggest difference in your relationships and hence in your sales results.

Empathy means you understand. Empathy does not necessarily mean you agree with the client; it simply means you know what they are talking about. Empathy is good. Empathy forces you to look at the situation/objection from the prospect's perspective. It forces you to pause and to think creatively for a solution or proper response.

To be an empathetic listener you must place yourself in the other person's shoes. This may sound easy but it is not, because before you put yourself in their shoes, you must take off your shoes. What I mean by that is that you must first drop or get rid of all of your preconceived ideas and assumptions. This is the most challenging part of being an empathetic listener, because it is not easy to drop all of your beliefs and go into a conversation with a totally open mind.

To be an empathetic listener you have to have a completely open mind such that you can actually experience what the other person has experienced. You must be able to see, feel and hear the experience as the other person does, from their point of view. You have to be open-minded and not bound by any beliefs or past experiences. You have to focus on listening with all of your emotions. You are living the experience as they have, not as you might have or would have.

An empathetic listener always places the prospect first, as it should be. An empathetic sales rep always sells more and makes more. Realize, as much as you work on being an empathetic listener, there are always obstacles that have to be overcome as well. Obstacles such as environmental noise, people walking by, telephones ringing and other interruptions. You have to learn to stay focused on the person you are communicating with at all times. If not, you lose.

Sometimes just missing out on a simple word, and not questioning that word for clarification, may cause you a problem. Over the years I have learned that people have different meanings for certain words based on their past experience. For example, in a lot of my workshops I ask the participants to identify 10 words that describe what the word education means to them. When we review each participant's words, you would think there would be some common words in the group, but that is not the case. Everyone has had a different experience relating to education and will describe it from their point of view. This is true of any experience or idea; therefore, it is important to sometimes question the words someone uses to ensure total understanding of where they are coming from.

A friend of mine had such an experience. Peter owns a number of service stations and hires at least four people per location. One day an Italian fellow came along and asked Peter for a job. At the time Peter had no opportunities and told him so. However, the Italian fellow persisted and after he mentioned that he had just arrived in Canada and needed work, Peter felt sorry for him and wanted to help. Peter asked him what he could do. The Italian fellow started listing a variety of jobs. As soon as Peter heard "painting," he seized the opportunity. He has a porch on the front of his house that his wife had been bugging him to get painted for over a year. Peter decided to hire the individual to paint the porch. He gave him directions to his house, told him the white paint was located behind the house in the shed, and asked him to paint the porch in front of the house with the white paint. Off he went.

At the end of the day the Italian fellow returned to the service station. Peter asked him how it was going. The Italian fellow responded that the job was done. Peter was surprised that he had gotten it done that quickly and asked, "You painted the porch in the front of the house white?" The Italian fellow responded, "Yes, but there is one thing that you should be aware of. That is not a Porsche you have in front of the house, that is a Maserati." Peter almost died on the spot.

Once you experience an incident like this, your communications skills improve dramatically. Peter's have. He now has the Italian fellow working with him full time, because it was actually a joke he played on Peter. However, Peter makes sure that everything he tells him is repeated back to him for clarity and full understanding. Don't wait until your red Maserati is painted white to learn to ask for clarity in order to have a full understanding of the words people use.

As you will note from the story above, there is a cost for not communicating effectively. If there are words used that you are not sure about, question them. If you are not sure the message you communicated is clearly understood, ask to have it repeated back to you. When communicating, you can miss out on important issues and you can easily lose the prospect's trust, which in turn will destroy the relationship. Be aware of what is being said; seek clarification and understanding.

Listening is a strong relationship builder, as is questioning. Questioning shows you care and want to learn, but only if you are listening. In order for you to be effective in sales you must first understand the prospect and where they are coming from. You need to hear them out, before they will ever hear you out. It is a matter of showing respect toward the prospect by listening and getting a full understanding of their experiences and needs.

Seek first to understand, if you really want to be understood.

Stephen Covey

It is only once you fully understand the prospect that you will be in a position to relate solutions back to them in a way they can understand. Therefore, stop telling and selling. Start by asking questions and listening empathetically. Listen beyond the spoken word. You will learn a lot more, gain a lot more respect and build lasting relationships. It is showing that you actually care about the prospect and their needs that makes the overall difference in a relationship.

Nobody cares how much you know until they know how much you care.

Cavett Robert

Let's take a look at some simple active listening techniques—parroting, paraphrasing, feeling feedback, and demonstrating listening through our body language.

Parroting is a listening technique whereby you repeat what the client has said. It demonstrates that you heard the exact words they said. **Paraphrasing** is similar but it is repeating what you heard in *your* words, not theirs. **Feeling feedback** demonstrates empathy by placing yourself in their scenario and feeling the way they must have felt, and expressing that feeling back to them. All three of these techniques can be used during your interaction with a prospect and can assist in demonstrating effective two-way communications. However, if your body language is not appropriate, these techniques are not very effective.

Body language plays a very important role in communications as it does in building rapport. Your body language speaks your mind. If you are looking at people walking by while having a conversation with an individual, what do you think your body is saying? Your body language, through your eye contact, is demonstrating that you are not listening to the person you are supposed to be communicating with and that you are more interested in what is going on around you than in listening to them.

Your body language always speaks your mind. Therefore when it comes to communication, which plays an important role in building relationships, we need to use our bodies to communicate effectively. Salespeople don't normally have a problem using their body when presenting or speaking, but many do when it comes to listening.

To listen effectively, we have to show that we are interested. That means we have to focus on the person speaking. You do that by maintaining eye contact and staying focused on them and on what they are saying. You lean in and use facial expressions and nods to demonstrate concern or interest or to show continued support. Use your body to show that you are listening—it will help you listen more effectively because you are aware of what you are doing and why.

I have witnessed many characteristics of good and poor listeners and would like to share the poor ones with you so that you can avoid them. If you have any of these characteristics, get rid of them! They are not doing you any good.

A poor listener is inattentive; has wondering eyes and poor posture; always interrupts; jumps to conclusions; finishes the speaker's sentence; changes the subject; writes everything down; does not give any response; is impatient; bad-tempered; fidgets with a pen, pencil or paper clip nervously.

We talked about the wandering eyes earlier; now let's look at each of the other characteristics. Poor posture is not sitting up and paying attention. If your arms are crossed and you are slouched down in your seat, you are certainly demonstrating that you are not interested. If you are constantly interrupting, jumping to conclusions or finishing sentences, as so many salespeople do, how do you think you are making the other person feel? Right—not at all important. You are actually making them feel you know it all and they are stupid. Is that what you want?

How do you feel when you are speaking about something and the other person changes the subject on you? Obviously they are not interested in what you are talking about and want to talk about something that is more interesting to them. Are you that type of self-centered person? If so, change, because in sales it is not about you, it is about the person in front of you.

In the chapter on asking questions I mentioned that you should bring only a notepad and a pen with you on your first sales call, but I didn't mention how you should be taking notes. If you are constantly writing everything down, you are not listening effectively. It is like being on vacation with a video camera, and you are so busy taking videos of everything that you are not really enjoying what you do see. The key is to write down brief words or important points only—trigger words. When the call is over and you have left the prospect, take a few minutes to debrief and elaborate on those trigger words for future reference. Also note anything else that is worth noting away from the prospect, not in front of them. When you are with the prospect, be there 110 percent.

In the last chapter you were advised to stay in control of the sales process by always asking questions and not giving any free consulting. In this chapter I mentioned that a poor listener does not give any response. There is a difference between not giving free consulting and not giving any response. Not giving a response shows you are not listening. By responding using one of the listening techniques above, you are showing you at least heard them or, even better, felt for them (using the feeling feedback technique). If you do not respond to what they have been saying, you have demonstrated that you were not listening and that you don't really care about what they have been saying.

If you are an impatient person, work on it. All good things come in time and you need to learn to master patience. Use your Monthly Monitor Chart and slowly you will master being patient, as I did. Don't ever lose your temper. When you do, you lose, always. Remember you can only control the things under your control, and your temper is something that is under your control. Seek to understand as opposed to blowing up. And when listening, don't fidget with things. They only take your focus away from where it should be.

On the following pages you will find a Listening Skills Assessment Worksheet for you to complete. Please be honest with yourself and identify the areas that you need to work on, then create an action plan to improve in each of the areas that you identified as weak.

Listening Skills Assessment Worksheet

Place check mark in the appropriate circle.

Always   Sometimes   Never

Concentration Skills

1. When I talk with others, my mind is completely absorbed by what they are saying, and it seldom wanders.   ◯ ◯ ◯

2. When in a conversation with others, I hold my comments until they are finished talking, even though my comments may have direct relevance to what they are saying at that time.   ◯ ◯ ◯

3. I do not let distractions like ringing telephones, busy street traffic, or other conversations in a room distract my attention from what someone is saying to me.   ◯ ◯ ◯

Always Sometimes Never

Acknowledgment Skills

4. When talking face to face or on the phone with someone, I acknowledge what has been said with "I understand" or "I see" or other comments that let the customer know I'm listening.   ◯ ◯ ◯

Research Skills

5. Whenever I talk with someone, I encourage the conversation and ensure that it will be a two-way flow of communication by asking open-ended questions, clarifying what I don't completely understand and giving appropriate feedback.   ◯ ◯ ◯

6. I let others know that I am listening and trying to understand what they are saying by using phrases like, "tell me more about that," or "can you give me an example?" or "then what?"   ◯ ◯ ◯

Sensing Skills

7. When I am talking with others, I read their body language as well as listen to their words, to fully interpret what they are telling me.   ◯ ◯ ◯

8. When talking with others, I try to read what is going on behind their spoken words by asking myself what they might be feeling, why they are saying what they are saying, and what the implications are.   ◯ ◯ ◯

Structuring Skills

9. Whenever I talk with others, I take either mental or written notes of the major idea, the key points, and the supporting points and/or reasons.   ◯ ◯ ◯

10. As I take my mental or written notes, I sequence—I listen for order or priority.   ◯ ◯ ◯

Areas that I need improvement in are:_____

_____

_____

_____

My action plan to improve in these areas is:_____

_____

_____

_____

The 7 Tips to Effective Listening

1. **Listen attentively**

    You must make the effort to concentrate on what the other person is saying, not on what you're going to say next.

    Be aware of your posture; the right posture enhances your ability to concentrate, eliminates distractions and communicates that you are listening attentively.

2. **Verify your understanding**

    Pause, think about what was said, and then think about what you will say.

    Repeat what was said using different words—without adding anything new or your interpretation.

    Describe what you think the other person said. This is a more complex approach because it requires you to add interpretation or inference—and it requires the other person to respond to those additions.

3. **Get confirmation that your verification was correct**

    The actual statement you make is only half of verifying.

    You must ask a question requesting the confirmation.

4. **Avoid appearing manipulative when seeking confirmation**

    Phrase your question in a neutral or positive way—for example, "Is that right?"

5. Seek clarification if you do not understand something

Don't wait.

Don't ignore your potential misunderstanding and risk letting it grow into an even larger misunderstanding.

6. Assume responsibility when a misunderstanding occurs

Don't appear to blame the other person—for any reason, no matter how ineffectively he or she seems to be communicating with you.

Remember that, as a salesperson, you want to build rapport. Making people feel foolish or at fault is not only rude but counterproductive.

7. Take advantage of nonverbal clues

Maintain eye contact and an open posture; face the other person squarely.

Be sensitive to the kind of nonverbal clues that you receive from the other person as you apply your active listening skills.

Verify the nonverbal "messages" that you receive.

Section C1 • Building Relationships

Lessons Learned _____

_____

_____

I Commit to Implement:

1. _____

_____

_____

2. _____

_____

_____

3. _____

_____

_____

I Need to Work on:

1. _____

_____

_____

2. _____

_____

_____

C2 • Qualifying Opportunities

You have learned how to build rapport in order to establish trust, how to ask questions in order to stay in control and how to listen effectively. You are now ready to move on to the next step in the system where you will have to apply all the questioning and listening skills you learned in order to qualify opportunities and further develop the relationship.

When you think of qualifying opportunities, what thoughts come to your mind?

Each salesperson has different opportunities to qualify during any day, and these opportunities come in a variety of forms, at different times of the day. If you are not ready to qualify these opportunities when they come along, you lose. So you must first understand what opportunities exist for your business and how to best qualify them so that you can take advantage of them when they do come along.

Take the time to identify the opportunities you already have to do business with people. These opportunities can come from walk-in traffic, listings in the Yellow Pages, advertising, your Web site, lead generation programs, database management programs, referrals, social functions, etc. List all avenues that bring potential prospects to your products or services.

Next, identify all other opportunities that you can benefit from. Opportunities like membership and active participation in associations, networking, trade shows, advertising supplements, sponsorships, partnering, etc. List as many as you can think of that will give you greater opportunities to meet and qualify prospects.

Next, identify opportunities that you can create that will help you increase your opportunities to meet and qualify prospects. You can create press releases based on all kinds of events—new product or service launches, new location, anniversaries, etc. You can write informative or educational articles on your industry, products or services that can be published in targeted magazines with your contact information. You can set up client appreciation, loyalty and referral programs. Get out of the box, brainstorm and list as many creative ways as possible to create new opportunities of meeting potential prospects.

Now that you have a complete list together, go back and rank them in order of importance. Which opportunities will give you the best return on your investment in time, energy and money? Next, lay out an action plan for the next year. Include in this plan a list of activities that will get you in front of as many potential prospects as possible. As you complete the implementation of each opportunity in the action plan, evaluate each of them for future reference.

You now have a list of opportunities that will get you out in front of prospects; all you have to do is qualify them. But what are you really qualifying them for? What do you consider to be the positive outcomes of a qualifying opportunity?

Simply taking the time to properly qualify a prospect, by asking intelligent questions is a value-added service that most salespeople don't offer. Too many salespeople just want to sell and forget about properly qualifying the prospect. Selling without qualifying is like a doctor who gives you a prescription without first diagnosing the problem.

When you have an opportunity to qualify a prospect, what is it that you really want? The answer you will get from most salespeople is "an order" or "a yes." But that is not the only answer you should be looking for when you qualify a prospect.

As a salesperson, your job is to qualify prospects. It is your responsibility to determine whether the prospect is qualified to do business with you, or not. In most cases, the opposite takes place. It is the prospect who qualifies the salesperson and their products or services. It is the salesperson who usually gets rejected, isn't it? In the ABC, 123 Sales Results System you are in control of the selling process, you will determine whether the prospect is qualified or not, and it is up to you to reject the prospect, not the other way around.

In other words, a **yes** is one positive outcome of a qualifying opportunity, but so is a **no**. When you realize how much time is wasted on people who are not qualified to buy, you will also realize that a no is also a positive outcome of a sales call. You also know that sales is a numbers game and you have to get through so many no's to get to a yes, so why not get through the no's quickly? Why would you want to waste your time on someone who is not qualified to buy from you?

If you don't get a yes, or a no, there are some other options. One of them is a **clear future** on what is going to happen next. A clear future is a clearly defined plan of action, committed to by the prospect, of the next steps in the process — steps that you agree are also important to proceed toward a yes or a no.

If you don't get a yes, a no or a clear future, you then have to find a **lesson learned**. A lesson learned means going back over the system and determining where you went wrong and what you can do better the next time to prevent the same thing from happening again.

The fifth and final positive outcome of an opportunity is to always ask for **a referral or an introduction**. Remember, one of your rights is to ask. If you don't ask, you don't get. It is your responsibility as a salesperson to ask. Make it a habit to always ask for a referral or an introduction from every qualifying opportunity, no matter what the outcome was.

The next question is, what do you do when you get in front of new prospects?

This is where the ABC, 123 Sales Results System comes into play. First we establish rapport to gain trust. We then need to qualify the prospect, through our questioning and listening skills, to determine whether the prospect is qualified or not. But qualified in what ways? This is what you as a salesperson must first understand. If you don't have your qualifiers identified, you will not succeed and you will fall into the buyer's system, leaving them in full control. Remember that it is your job as a salesperson to qualify prospects, not the other way around.

To qualify a prospect we must first set the parameters of our meeting to eliminate surprises and create an environment of trust, honesty and openness. This is where you create additional trust and make the client feel more comfortable with you. Too many salespeople don't do this and leave the prospect feeling uncomfortable and nervous throughout the whole meeting.

Once the prospect is comfortable, you then need to question them to determine whether there are any buying motivators for your products or services. You need to know what questions you must ask them here to fully uncover three or four problems or buying motivators. If they have no reason to buy, they are not going to buy; therefore they are not qualified, at present, to buy.

However, if there are reasons to buy, you need to find out if they have any money to pay for the products or services you may have that could help them. You also need to know when they will be making that decision to buy and who will be making that decision. These are all qualifiers— answers that you need before you can give any information away.

Once you have all of this information you can then summarize and determine whether there is an opportunity to do business or not. If you can solve their buying motivators or problems, within their budget and time frame, you then have a qualified opportunity. If you can't there is no sense in proceeding— the prospect is simply not qualified to receive a presentation. You abort, maintain the relationship and seek out referrals and introductions.

Let's now take a closer look at each of these qualifying areas of:

1. Setting the parameters;
2. Qualifying by uncovering buying motivators, financial ability and decision-making process;
3. Summarizing.

C2.1 • Setting the Parameters

Setting the parameters of a meeting is not new. It exists in all professions, including sports. It is simply setting the ground rules as to how the parties are going to interact during the course of the meeting or play. The nice thing about setting the parameters is that it eliminates surprises and makes everyone feel much more comfortable.

Naturally, to do this you may have to change your traditional ways and realize something important right up front. Earlier in this book we talked about the most important person in the world. I am sure you agreed that it was you. However, when we are with a prospect, who do you believe the most important person is?

Hopefully you responded with the prospect being the most important person. Remember one thing, that without a prospect you have no opportunity for doing business. Therefore, when you are with a prospect, make sure they are treated as the most important person in the world, and you can do this by including them in setting the parameters.

Let's understand your first objective as simply to meet with a prospect to determine whether there is an opportunity to do business or not. Whatever the outcome, your objective would still be to establish a relationship. Therefore you still follow the system and build rapport. Once you feel you have established rapport and the customer is feeling comfortable with you, you are ready to get down to business and set the parameters.

But what parameters should be set, you ask? Good question; let's start by asking permission to ask questions and take notes. Then put yourself in the shoes of the prospect, and ask yourself what would make anyone feel comfortable in the meeting. There are a few things that make most people more comfortable, like knowing the amount of time allocated to the meeting, the objective or outcomes, the agenda and/or possible next steps. But there are also some other very important parameters that need to be set for a sales meeting.

The real secret in setting these parameters is to not tell the prospect what the parameters are but to ask the prospect what they should be. When they are the prospect's answers, he or she owns them and will respect them. If you tell them, they are your parameters, not theirs. It is most important that they feel they are taking ownership of the meeting at the outset. It has to be their ideas. This is how they will feel they are in control. You will still have an opportunity to add yours, but only after they have stated theirs.

You start by simply asking a question: *John, you probably want to know a lot about my product or service and I am okay with you asking me questions. However, I also want to know a lot about your business; do you mind if I ask you some questions? Is it okay if I also take some notes as we go?*

Then you can proceed to confirm the amount of time that has been set aside for the meeting. For example: *John, how much time have you set aside for our meeting today?* Hopefully the answer will be what was previously agreed to, or more time. If so answer, *great!* If less time is provided, question why and reschedule for the amount of time you need if there is not enough time, or try to do the little bit that you can in the amount of time provided to qualify the prospect. Don't try to do something you know requires a larger amount of time. If you try to do it in less time, you will probably lose.

Now that you have confirmed the amount of time available to you, you can simply ask the prospect what their objectives, or outcomes, for the meeting are, and the agenda. Remember that objectives and outcomes are the end results of a meeting and you are striving to find out *their* end result. For example: *What objective (or end result) should we work toward during the 30 minutes we have together? Did you want to set an agenda?* If so, let them lead the way. Add in your agenda items as you go. You may also want to ask, *What would be the next step if we don't get to all the items listed on the agenda?* Always strive to get a clear future and a commitment from the prospect every step along the way.

A word of caution—however you ask the questions or lead the prospect, be yourself. Ask questions your way and have some fun. Don't take qualifying too seriously. Buyers are stressed enough as it is. Try to inject some humor along the way. The more they laugh the more the barriers come down.

You have just confirmed or learned some obvious things in setting parameters for a meeting. Now, let's take it a step closer to the real world of sales. One of the biggest fears prospects have of salespeople is that they are going to sell them something, something they probably don't want. How do we get around this fear, so that they can let their barriers down, have some fun and be more relaxed and receptive?

Traditional sales training has always told us to go for a "yes." In sales you know that you cannot satisfy everyone's needs and that your responsibility is to also reject clients, and that they can also reject you.

As a matter of fact, you are probably getting more no's than yes's as it is. We have already agreed that a no is a positive outcome of a qualifying opportunity. We also know that it takes many no's to get a yes. Therefore, let's take control, change our attitude and go for the opposite. Let's go for a "no" instead of a "yes." By doing so, what do you think will happen with the prospect? Do you think their barriers may come down, they may have some fun and they may be more relaxed and receptive?

Simply say something like, *At this stage, I don't know if I can help you or not, but if I can't are you okay with me telling you no I can't help you? The same applies to you. I already know I can't solve everyone's problems. If you feel I can't help you could you please tell me no, as I am okay with no?*

Again, be yourself and use your words, not mine. All you want to do is make the prospect feel comfortable with the idea that you may not be able to help them, that you are not there to sell them something they don't want or need. You are there to ask them questions to determine whether there is a fit or not and if not, you will tell them so, and/or it is okay for them to also tell you no, because you are okay with a no. But you had better be sure your attitude *is* okay with a no.

Once we have established that saying no is okay we can then move to the opposite side of the coin, something like, *However, if you feel I can help you, you can say yes. My only concern is that I don't want to waste your time and I am sure you don't want to waste mine. Would it be okay with you if we work on a honest yes-no basis and eliminate things like 'think it over,' which usually means no?*

You have now set the parameters of working on an honest yes/no basis to which "think it over," one of a salesperson's biggest obstacles, no longer exists. The same process can work for you in eliminating common objections, interruptions and all other obstacles that you face in sales interactions.

Dealing with common and major objections is one of the biggest fears of a salesperson. Most salespeople feel they have to justify and end up replying to objections. The best way to deal with a common objection is to deal with it right up front, in the setting up of the parameters. Simply take your most common or major objection and ask if it is going to be a problem. If it is, thank the prospect for their time and move on. Don't waste any more of your time. If you had a millionaire's attitude you wouldn't be sticking around and you know it. If it is not a problem, you just eliminated the objection (an excuse for not doing business with you) from coming up again.

Now let me give you a personal example of how I overcame serious interruptions at a conference in Pakistan, where other speakers and I were speaking to over 400 business people. Fortunately, I was one of the last speakers to perform so I was able to witness the problem. I then realized I had to set the parameters and demonstrate how this simple technique can also work for the participants in the audience.

On day one of the conference there were three speakers on various topics, each speaking for 90 minutes. At the beginning of the conference, and after each speaker, the emcee would get up and tell everyone to turn off their cellular phones and beepers as it was disturbing others and causing interruptions. Nothing ever changed and the cellulars and beepers continued to sound off.

On day two the same thing happened. The emcee got up and asked everyone to turn off their cellulars and beepers. I was then introduced and began my talk on sales. I always like to open by asking questions to get to a point. The point I wanted to make with this audience was the importance of sales, and it came across well. I then went into my overview of what I was going to cover over the next 90 minutes and asked how we could retain the information I going to share with them. They answered the way I wanted them to—apply it within 48 hours, take notes, share it with others, etc.

Then I proceeded to eliminate the interruptions caused by cellulars and beepers. I walked off the stage down into the audience. I went up to a gentleman and asked him the following: *Have you ever been in the midst of a conversation where you are about to make an important point and the phone rings?* He answered yes, and I asked what happened. He replied that he lost his focus, his concentration. I then turned to another person somewhere behind me and asked him, *What we can do so that we don't lose our focus or concentration today?* He replied with "turn off our cellulars and beepers." "Great," I said, and then went to another person and asked if she agreed. She responded yes, and I asked *and if one goes off how should that person be penalized?* She replied with, "Have them take their call on stage." I then ran up on stage and asked the full audience, *Is there anyone here who disagrees with the penalty—if your cellular or beeper sounds, you take the call on stage?* Not one hand went up, and guess what—not one cellular phone or beeper sounded during my presentation.

After my talk there was one more speaker. The emcee thanked the audience for turning off their cellulars and beepers and told them to keep them off. The emcee did not learn my technique. The audience had set the parameters with me and not the emcee or the next speaker. Unfortunately, the phones were ringing again.

Setting the parameters is a standard in all of my meetings and training sessions. It gives the participants ownership, not to mention involvement, in the program. There is no particular order to setting up any of these parameters. Just make it a point to address the ones that matter most to you and your prospect, and others as need be, in some way. Know what parameters you want to work under. Ask the right questions in a way that gets the other person to tell you what you want to hear. Remember that to have the parameters respected, it must be the other person's idea—they have to own it.

Summary

Set the parameters by getting the prospect involved.
Get permission to ask questions and take notes.
Confirm time, objective, agenda, end result.
Go with "no" or "yes" and eliminate "think it over."
Avoid interruptions.
Deal with major or common objections.

C2.2.1 • Qualifying by Uncovering Buying Motivators

What are buying motivators? Buying motivators are the reasons someone buys something. Your job as a salesperson is to uncover these reasons in advance so that you can facilitate the buying process for the prospect. Once you know the reasons, the rest is easy, but uncovering the reasons is easier said than done. First, let's understand why people buy.

People buy for emotional reasons. They justify their purchase intellectually. Features and benefits are not emotional and do not belong early in the sales process. There is a place for them and it is at the end of the process when you are providing a prescription to a decision maker who is ready to make a buying decision. Therefore, stop those feature and benefit dumps. Your job at this stage of the process is to stay in control and qualify the prospect by uncovering their buying motivators.

There are two emotional reasons (buying motivators) people purchase something. One is to eliminate a pain and the other is to gain a pleasure. Which one of the two emotions do your products and/or services satisfy? Do they eliminate pain, do they provide a pleasure or do they fit into both categories?

For example, if you sell real estate, you can be selling pain relief and/or pleasure depending on the prospect's needs. Pain relief is providing housing to someone who is desperately in need, while pleasure could be selling in a prestigious resort community.

You have heard it before—no pain, no gain. This is true for sales; if you cannot find the prospect's pain, or emotional buying motivators, you will gain no sale. You can find someone's pain or pleasure by simply asking questions, questioning the answer and, of course, listening for cues. But first you must learn which questions to ask. The best questions are those that can get a prospect talking openly about a topic that will identify problems you have solutions for. Always start with an open-ended question in the area where you want to dig deep.

The easiest way to do this is to create a three-column chart, like the one following, and in the "Solutions" column on the left identify and list the solutions that your products or services provide. In the "Problems" column, list the problems that each solution solves. Then in the third column, "Topic Questions," list the open-ended questions that need to be asked to uncover the problems that you have solutions for. There is no sense asking questions to uncover problems that you have no solutions for, is there?

Solutions	Problems	Topic Questions
1. _____	1. A. _____	1. A. _____
_____	B. _____	B. _____
_____	C. _____	C. _____

2. _____	2. A. _____	2. A. _____
	B. _____	B. _____
	C. _____	C. _____
3. _____	3. A. _____	3. A. _____
	B. _____	B. _____
	C. _____	C. _____

Being prepared in advance and knowing what questions to ask is half the battle. The other half is listening to the answers and questioning the answers to find out how bad the problem is or how much the pain hurts. Before proceeding, complete the chart to the best of your ability.

Next, identify the information you need from each of the problems. These are the fact-finding types of questions you read about in an earlier section. These are the answers you need that will help you to position your solution to solve their problems.

Once you have gathered the factual information you need, you then need to dig a little deeper. You need to ask questions to get the prospect to analyze those problems in depth. Questions such as:

How long have you had this problem?

What have you done to fix it?

Why hasn't it worked?

How much is this problem costing you or the organization?

How does this affect you?

How does this make you feel personally?

By asking these in-depth questions, you will be going deeper into the problem, deeper than most salespeople have ever gone before. Take a closer look at those questions. The answers can give you valuable information on timing, competition, what didn't work and why, how much the problem is costing the organization and what the real buying motivators are—both corporate and personal. At the same time you will be drawing out real personal emotions.

Personal emotions are what you have to draw out and where you have to get to. These are the strongest of all emotions. People will always solve their own problems before they solve someone else's. Find out the real personal problems and how it makes them feel and you will have a personal buying motivator in support of the corporate buying motivator. Once you find out the personal buying motivators, your chances of success have greatly increased.

Once you have brought the prospect to a realization of their personal buying motivators, reasons or pains and how it makes them feel, don't dwell on it. Quickly move on to identifying other problems by asking another one of the open-ended questions you identified above to get them talking about other problems. Follow the process through again.

Once you have reviewed and identified three to five problems, you probably have enough information to determine whether you have any buying motivators or not. If you do, proceed to the next step. If not, don't be afraid to abort. Remember, you set the parameter of not wasting their time and telling them you can't help them if you felt you couldn't. Respect what you agreed upon.

Again, this is not for you to tell, but to ask. The prospect needs to uncover these things for himself or herself. You are there to guide them through the self-discovery process, not to tell them or make it simple for them. You should already know what talking too much will cost you.

Summary

Get and keep the prospect talking.

Find the emotional problem.

Dig deep.

Question the answer.

Seek clarification and full understanding.

Find the personal problems and associated costs.

C2.2.2 • Qualifying by Uncovering Financial Ability

Now that you have identified three to five buying motivators and believe that you can provide the prospect with pain relief through your solutions, you have decided to proceed with the qualification process. The next step in the process is to identify the prospect's financial ability—if they have any money available, and how much, to solve the problems identified. This is also the time to discuss any and all financial issues that may be of concern.

A lot of people have problems talking about money because they were told that money is a personal matter and should never be discussed. Well, you are now in business and payment for a sale is important, is it not? If you don't discuss financial issues, how will you know what they can afford as a solution, or if your solution fits within their budget or if you will even get paid?

To enter into this step simply review the problems identified and ask the prospect this simple question: *Do you have a budget set aside to cover these problems?*

Naturally they can answer yes or no. If they answer no, simply ask, *How do you intend to proceed?* Shut up and wait for their answer—then question the answer and make a decision on how you want to proceed, whether to abort or whether to come back at a later date.

If they answered yes, simply ask, *Could you share that budget with me in round numbers?* "Sharing" is partnering and "round numbers" is less intimidating. These two key words should always be used when uncovering financial ability. If the prospect provides you with the information you are looking for, great. However, if they answered yes, *but I can't share that information with you,* how would you respond?

Now you will have to revert to price ranges. For example, you could say something like: *Well, John, we have solutions in a variety of price ranges from $1,000 to $10,000. Would you be in the $1,000 to $5,000 range or the $5,000 to $10,000 range?* Your job would be to narrow down the budget number to a point where you have some sort of idea of how much money is available to solve the problems. You can even ask questions on how they budgeted for similar purchases in the past.

Remember you are still gathering information, not giving it. However, if in the process you are forced to reveal your pricing, always reveal your highest price, as it is easier to come down in price than it is to increase it later.

Also in the process you may uncover that there is not enough money in the budget to solve the client's problems or to pay for your solution. You will then have to make more decisions before moving on. You can decide to take the little that there is and do something with it, service the client, build the relationship and be in a position to take it all when more funds are available. Or you can reveal to the client that you cannot help them within the budget that is available. Whatever you decide to do, be open and honest as agreed and maintain the relationship.

You may have other financial issues that need to be dealt with—issues that relate to terms or methods of payment, for example. This is the time and place to discuss them. Don't leave any financial questions or issues on the table. Deal with them all now.

Summary

Review the three to five problems identified.
Ask, "Have you got a budget set aside?"
No—"How do you plan on proceeding?"
Yes—"Would you mind sharing it with me in round numbers?"
Use price ranges or bracketing.
Address all financial issues.

C2.2.3 • Qualifying by Uncovering the Decision-making Process

You have now identified three to five buying motivators, discussed all financial issues and know there is a budget available and the approximate amount, and still believe that you can provide them with pain relief, within their budget. You have decided to proceed with the qualification process. The next step in the process is to uncover the prospect's decision-making process.

You start this step by reviewing the problems and budget that were previously discussed and simply ask: *John, when will a decision be made to solve these problems?* "When" is one of the most important questions that need to be asked about making decisions. If the answer is now, great! But if they don't know or if they say in six months, what would you do then?

Obviously you would question their answers and get more in-depth information. Hopefully you will realize that it is also not wise to give a presentation until they are ready to make a decision. Why else would you give a presentation?

The other important question to ask is: *John, who besides yourself is involved in the decision-making process?* The important words here are "besides yourself." Quite often we think we are speaking with the decision maker, but in reality this person may only be able to say no. Your job is to uncover all people involved in the decision-making process. By including the individual you are speaking to, you are stroking them and making them feel important. Omit them and you are insulting them. Don't ever insult a prospect. By the way, you can also ask how similar decisions were made in the past, as history does repeat itself.

Should other people be involved, you have to find out who they are and go through the whole sales process again, with each decision maker, starting with building rapport. You will soon learn that everyone is different — has different dominant senses, different buying motivators and even different budgets. You will have to appeal to them all, even if a committee is involved.

However, what can you do if you can't get in front of the committee? Well, then you will need someone to represent you to that committee. You will have to uncover the questions that the committee would ask and then present and coach the individual that will be representing you. Make sure that person has as strong a belief in your solutions as you do.

Keep in mind that there could be many other people involved in influencing decisions too. These people could be consultants, agencies or even outside suppliers or friends. Find out who they are and if you can appeal to them as if they were decision makers as well. Follow the ABC, 123 Sales Results System and remember that the more you know the better off you will be.

Summary

Review problems and budget.

Ask, "When will you be making a decision?"

Ask, "Who *besides yourself* is involved in the decision-making process?"

What about others—committees, agencies, etc.?

C2.3 • Summarizing

You have built rapport with the client and established trust. You have now qualified the prospect on buying motivators, financial ability and decision making. You asked a lot of questions, got a lot of answers and listened effectively. You remained in control of the process and have not revealed any significant information on your products and services. You are now in a position to review your findings with the prospect and to make a decision on the next step.

Before summarizing ask yourself the following questions:

1. Does the prospect have a need?
2. Are your products or services able to satisfy the prospect's need?
3. Is the prospect able to buy?
4. Is the prospect ready to buy?
5. Is the prospect willing to buy . . . *from you*?

Based on the answers to these questions you will have a good idea where you stand in the sales process. You either have the potential of a sale and proceed with a presentation, or you don't and you consider your options on how to proceed. Whatever you decide to do, maintain the relationship for future development, introductions and referrals.

Let's pretend the prospect is qualified and you decide to proceed. There are two ways to summarize. One way is to ask the prospect to review what was discussed to ensure clarification. The other is for you to review, or summarize, all of your findings. You identify the buying motivators, the budget allocated and the decision-making timing and people involved. You then ask for confirmation of all of your summary findings.

It is important to note that you should be using the prospect's words and relating to the prospect's dominant sense at this stage of the process, not the words of the system or the words that you feel comfortable with. You have to be able to communicate with the prospect in the way they want to be communicated with. You also want to seek their confirmation on buying motivators, budget and decision making, or obtain any clarifications, before moving on.

You want to also uncover any other issues that could prevent you from doing business. After obtaining their confirmation on the summary simply ask, *Are there any other issues, problems or reasons that would prevent us from doing business?* If no, great—proceed. If yes, find out what the issues, problems or reasons are, question the answer and proceed, or abort, accordingly. This is the time to defuse any bombs before they go off.

Next you want to move into the prescription phase, but before you do that you want to reinforce one of the parameters that was set at the beginning of the meeting. The parameter is the yes/no decision. You could do that by saying something like, *John, at the beginning of our meeting we agreed to be honest with each other and to give yes/no answers. I believe I can solve your problems within your budget and timing. I am now prepared to provide you with a solution. At the end of my presentation are you still okay with giving me a yes or no answer?*

You must receive a commitment here before you proceed. If you don't you could be wasting your time doing a presentation. Why would you even want to do a presentation if you are not going to get a yes or no answer?

Once you do get the commitment, ask the prospect what their presentation expectations are and how much time they can allocate to the presentation. You should also confirm the location of the presentation and the resources that may be needed.

All too often salespeople provide their canned presentation and dictate the time. Remember, we are here for the prospect and without them we have nothing. The presentation is for them, so that you can get a sale. Let's at least meet, or still better, exceed their presentation expectations. The only way we can do that is to ask and to prepare accordingly.

Remember that not all the steps in the sales process have to be completed at one meeting. Each meeting can be a step within itself or the process can run over several meetings depending on the complexity of the account. The important part is to continuously review your parameters and findings at each meeting, making the appropriate adjustments as need be. Constantly seek confirmation and clarification. When in doubt, don't proceed; question the doubt. You are the one in control of the process.

Summary

Summarize buying motivators, financial ability, decision making.
Confirm a yes/no response prior to presentation.
Use the prospect/client's words and dominant sense.
Ask for other issues or problems before proceeding.
Know the client's presentation expectations and time allocated.

Section C.2 • Qualifying Opportunities

Lessons Learned _____

_____

_____

I Commit to Implement:

1. _____

_____

_____

2. _____

_____

_____

3. _____

_____

_____

I Need to Work on:

1. _____

_____

_____

2. _____

_____

_____

C3 • Prescribing Solutions

You have built rapport and obtained the prospect's trust. You set the parameters; you uncovered the buying motivators, the financial ability and the decision-making process. You summarized your findings, obtained confirmation and got a commitment to proceed with a presentation to the decision makers, after which you will receive a yes or no answer. You now have a qualified prospect, or a hot one, about to turn into a customer. Otherwise you would not be at this step in the process.

The objective of this step in the process is to take everything you learned and to come up with a prescription—a customized solution based on your products and services—to solve the prospect's problems within their budget and time frames. This means you are to present solutions specific to the problems identified and no more. Your job is to now get the sale based on the information gathered. Sell today based on that information and get the sale. You can always go back and up-sell or cross-sell once you have the sale. For now stay focused on getting the sale by addressing solutions specific to the problems identified.

To make this clearer, think about your last visit to a doctor. As a salesperson you are really no different. The doctor greets you and conducts a little small talk to make you feel comfortable. You do the same when you are building rapport with the prospect. The doctor tells you what he is going to do and then starts to ask you a lot of questions to identify the exact problem. You ask the prospect how they would like to proceed and you too start to ask a lot of questions to identify the exact problem. Once the doctor finds the problem, he summarizes the findings and usually provides you with a prescription to solve that specific problem. You are to do the same. When you ask the doctor about other issues, they usually book another meeting. You should do the same.

You are a professional, no different from a doctor, a dentist or a lawyer. When you conduct yourself as a professional you gain respect. Respect from all suspects, prospects, "hot ones" and clients is what you should be aiming for. You do this by setting some professional standards for yourself and following through on them. Ask questions, listen, be honest, stay focused and develop relationships, before you present.

This is the step in the process where you do finally get to present. You get to present solutions to the problems, within the budget and time constraints that you uncovered, to the person or people who are ready and able to make a yes or no decision. This is the step where you will also let the buyer buy and where you will follow through to maintain and develop the relationship.

C3.1 • Presentations

Presentation skills are a must for everyone, even if you are not in sales, as you must be able to present and sell yourself and your ideas to others. But before we get into the actual presentation we must realize that great presentations start with preparation. It is in the preparation that you can make a difference.

Preparation, when following the ABC, 123 Sales Results System, started early in the process through the gathering of all the pertinent in-depth information, not just surface information. You even prepared in advance of the call and identified the questions that you needed answers to. Too many salespeople don't prepare and don't dig deep enough before they present. They are impatient and anxious to get the sale and usually end up losing it because they didn't prepare to dig deep enough, listen or gather enough pertinent information—information that you now know is crucial if you are going to get the prospect to buy your solution. The more information you can gather, the easier this preparation and presentation step will be for you.

When preparing for your presentation or proposal, consider all the information you gathered on audience physiology, tonality, words, dominant senses, parameters, buying motivators, finances, decisions, presentation expectations, resources and time allocated, etc. When doing a presentation or a proposal all of these elements have to be reviewed and confirmed, including the confirmation of a yes or no answer after the presentation, before providing your solution to the decision maker(s). That is why the previous step of summarizing is so important. Let's also refer to this as the beginning of a presentation or proposal—a review of all of your findings to ensure nothing has changed and confirmation of a yes or no answer at the end of the presentation.

Next we get into the second component of a presentation, the middle. This is where your solutions come in. You have to decide on what solutions you will be providing to solve the specific problems identified— solutions that will not only solve the problems identified, but will solve them within the budget and time constraints. You also have to identify the features and benefits you will present and how you will present them in each participant's dominant sense, while exceeding their presentation expectations in the time frame allocated. This is the crucial step in a presentation. You have to demonstrate or prove how your products or services will solve their problems or give them the pleasures they are looking for.

In addition you have to consider your opening and closing remarks. What can you say that will capture the individual's, or audience's, attention on opening and how will you close off? For now, don't be concerned about your closing remarks, as that will be covered in the next section when we discuss letting the buyer buy.

As for your opening remarks, there are several ways to go about it. You can open with a question or two relating to the solving of a problem identified, use a quote, or simply state a related fact. Your opening statement should be powerful to capture their attention, and then followed with a greeting and an overview of what will be following. Tell them what you are going to do, so there are no surprises. Then you can begin your presentation.

Let's take a closer look at the presentation itself. You are prepared and you arrived earlier than scheduled. You set up, test equipment and greet everyone by shaking hands and matching their handshake as they arrive. You provide an opening statement, verbally greet them, provide an overview of how you are going to proceed with the presentation and confirm a yes or no answer at the end of the presentation.

You then proceed and review all the pertinent information you gathered and confirm that nothing has changed. If things have changed, consider your options and react accordingly. Once confirmed, you proceed by asking a simple question like, *From the problems identified, which one would you like to provide a solution to first?* This technique invites the prospect to get involved. The answer you get will probably be their biggest problem. You then proceed to provide a solution to that problem. This is where all those features and benefits you have learned about your products and services come out, but mention only those that are relevant to the specific problem at hand.

Keep in mind that you are presenting to the decision maker(s) and you must be communicating to them in a way that is appealing to their dominant sense while using their words, tonality and physiology as best you can. You are there for them, not you, right?

The same applies to proposals. The main advantage you have when making proposals is to first deliver a proposal as a draft. A proposal follows the same lines as a presentation with the same beginning, middle and end. The difference is that the words are written, not spoken. The idea behind a draft is to partner with a prospect. When you prepare a proposal and give it to someone, it is your ideas, not theirs, therefore you own it, not them. By getting their agreement to your submitting a draft proposal you are giving them a chance to input and take part ownership. Your job is to ensure you get them to add, correct or adjust something in that proposal. As soon as they incorporate something into the proposal, they take ownership. The proposal goes from being "yours" to being "ours." It should be your objective to always partner with a prospect where possible.

Let's go back to the presentation. After presenting a solution to the prospect's biggest problem you want to obtain agreement as to its solution. You can do this by asking if this solution satisfies that problem. If you did your job right, the answer should be yes. You can then confirm that yes by asking, "100 percent?" or if doing a visual presentation, place a check mark next to that problem. If you get a no or not 100 percent, ask how it doesn't satisfy or what is missing. Ask questions to seek out what is missing or why they responded the way they did. If in doubt, take the blame as if you did something wrong and seek out where you went wrong. Resolve any and all issues relating to this problem and its solution before moving on. Once you got confirmation of 100 percent, move on by asking, *What problem would you like me to address next?*

You then proceed to provide solutions to that next problem using all the relevant product or service features and benefits and repeat the 100 percent confirmation process. If you have fewer than four problems to which you have to provide solutions, you may want to proceed to measure their interest. If you have more than four, continue this process until you feel the customer is on board. If you are not sure how your presentation is being received, you can also proceed to measure their interest. Measuring someone's interest can save you time and get to the real issues. It is in the measuring process that we allow the buyer to buy.

Summary

The purpose of a presentation is to get a sale.

Always present in the other person's point of view and dominant sense.

There are three parts of a presentation—beginning (summary), middle (solutions), and end (letting the customer buy).

Open by getting their attention.

After the beginning ask, "Which problem would you like me to provide a solution for first?"

Provide a solution to the problem within their budget and time frames. This is where the features and benefits of your products and/or services belong.

C3.2 • Letting the Buyer Buy

The Interest Technique is a simple method that you can use to measure the level of interest the prospect has in doing business with you by the way your solutions solve his or her problems. It can save time and reveal concerns or issues that may have been overlooked or not previously discussed.

The Interest Technique also lets the buyer buy. Consider it as a trial close if you like, as it does lead to the close.

The Interest Technique is based on the common scale of 1 to 10 and can be presented, in your words and the prospect's dominant sense, something like: *On a scale of 1 to 10 where do you see [visual] yourself? One you don't see using our product [and/or services], 10 you are already there seeing us as your supplier. Where do you see yourself on the scale?*

Naturally, you can get any number as a response. For a rating of under six, you have to accept the blame and ask where did you go wrong and use this information to take corrective action or take it as a lesson learned. Mind you, if you followed the process from the beginning, asked the right questions, questioned the answers, dug deep, listened and are presenting solutions to the problems identified, within budget and time constraints, this should not be happening, right? But if you did skip some of the steps in the process or did not dig deep enough, expect this to happen.

You should, however, be getting ratings above 7. Any rating between a 7 and a 9 is a good sign and warrants the question, *What will it take to get you to a 10?* Listen to their response and give them what it will take to get them to a 10. Then re-affirm their rating again. It should be a 10. If it is only a 9, have some fun and say something like *John, is it possible that you really work on a scale of 1 to 9 and 10 doesn't exist?* Shut up and wait for their answer, which could be something like a simple giggle confirming you are right.

The hot prospect is now committed. All you have to do now is ask the closing question, which can be as simple as *What would you like me to do next?* Again, shut up and wait for a response. The hot prospect's (buyer) response could be something like, let's complete the paperwork, sign an agreement, or process the purchase order. Their response is where they buy.

If you followed and implemented the ABC, 123 Sales Results System, you will experience how quickly you can qualify prospects, shorten your sales cycle, stay in control and experience this unbelievable and most rewarding phase of the process. There is no greater feeling than having someone buy from you through this self-discovery process.

But it doesn't end here. You now have a client and that client has expectations of you, your organization and its products and services.

You have to remain proactive, retain the account and develop it for more business.

Summary

Use the *Interest Technique*: 1 to 10 scale—1 no, 10 yes.
Rating under 6—Take the fault, take corrective actions.
Ratings 7 to 9 —What must I do to get you to a 10?
Close by asking, "What would you like me to do next?"
Let the buyer buy.

C3.3 • Account Retention and Development

You have gone through the process of converting a prospect to a "hot one" to a client. You now have a buyer who has agreed to purchase your products or service. You, or they, prepare all the paperwork and have it all signed off. However, you may have some concerns that you need to deal with. Concerns about back-outs or cancellations or how your competitor, from whom you are taking away business, will react. If you have any concerns about any of these, or other issues, now is the time to address them.

Similarly, as a buyer, how do you feel after making a large purchase? Think about the last time you purchased a product or service of similar value to that which you are selling. Did you have any doubts about your purchase? Did you discuss it with others to re-affirm your purchase? Did you ever back out of a deal you made?

It is common for purchasers to have what is called *buyer's remorse*, especially after purchasing large-ticket items. Is it possible that your buyer may experience buyer's remorse, consider backing out or turning back to your competitor, from whom you took the business, for a lower price or some other concession?

These are issues salespeople face on an ongoing basis. You have to be aware of these issues and be able to address them now, while you are in front of the client, as you may not be able to get back in front of them once they back out. So let's take a look at how we can deal with them one at a time.

If the client had to make a concession to do business with you and there is a possibility of a back-out, select a minor concession or objection that might have come up somewhere in the process. Then ask if that concession, or any other issues, would cause them to back out of the deal. All you are trying to do is raise any issues that could lead to a back-out while they are in front of you. If they don't raise any issues, you have their commitment that they wouldn't back out. If they do, deal with them immediately.

If you are taking business away from one of your competitors and are concerned that the client may go back to them, deal with it now, while you are in front of them. Simply ask them how they think your competitor, or their existing supplier, will react when they hear the news about you switching suppliers. Ask the buyer what they think that supplier would do to keep the business or get it back? Ask them if they would go back. Address any issues in order to get their commitment to staying with you. Also you may want to provide the client with some coaching on how to deal with their existing supplier when they do call and offer lower prices or other concessions. Think about the things you can do to add some extra value and build on the relationship you started. You may even volunteer to call their existing supplier and notify them for the client. Whatever you do, help the client however you can and get a commitment from them that they will respect and follow though on the agreement you made with them.

The next issue to cause back-outs is buyer's remorse. Buyer's remorse usually sets in after the sale is made and you are gone. With buyer's remorse they go through three phases. First the buyer may experience some doubt and will then tell others of their purchase, looking for feedback, or external verification, as to whether or not they made the right decision. Based on all the feedback they obtained they will then proceed with the original decision or change their mind and cancel the sale. If you are selling products or services where buyer's remorse is an issue, again you must deal with it while the customer is in front of you.

One of the best ways I have found to deal with buyer's remorse is to tell people third-party stories. Third-party stories help the client know there are others, like them, that went through the same process as they did and what happened to them. They went home, told their friends, and their friends said . . . and then we got the call and they forgot and the sale was reconfirmed. Naturally, third-party stories have positive outcomes. Share those positive outcome stories with clients who you think will go through buyer's remorse and ask them if it will be an issue or not with them. If so, deal with it then. If not, you have their commitment that it will not be an issue later.

With all of these issues, and others, you are just getting commitments by asking questions. In a way it is very similar to what you did when you set the parameters before starting the meeting. You have now set the parameters of what can happen, how to deal with it and how to proceed from this point on.

Now the meeting is coming to an end. You must know what the expectations of the client are and be prepared to exceed them. You should also ask for a referral or an introduction before leaving and let the client know when he will be hearing from you next. The sale is complete and you are leaving with commitments, and referrals or introductions.

You should now take the time to determine what steps to take next to maintain and develop the relationship. After you make a purchase what are some of the things you would like to see happen? Sure, you want your product or service delivered as scheduled, but what else?

This is where you have the opportunity to stand out and make another significant difference. Come up with a list of things you can do that go beyond the verbal thank you. Show the client that you do appreciate their business, and go the extra mile for them, however you can. Think of ways to maintain the relationship, to stay in contact and to be considered as a friend or referred to as "my" supplier by your client. Don't think too much about it; just do it!

Very few individuals take the five minutes it requires to acknowledge or thank someone with a personal handwritten note of recognition for their patronage. If you truly want to make your customers or potential customers feel appreciated and special, then take the time to write and send a personal note. It may truly be the one extraordinary customer service step that brings the client back again and again.

There are numerous reasons that deserve to be acknowledged by a personal note, or even an e-mail message. Some of these are a purchase, a person taking the time to meet with you, a luncheon meeting, a presentation, a lead or a referral, a social or sporting event, a networking opportunity, and/or a gift. Make it a practice to show your appreciation and you will certainly make yourself memorable.

Make an effort also to stay in communication with the client. Follow up to ensure everything went according to plan. Always be proactive. Find reasons to communicate with them on an ongoing basis. Go beyond what is standard or required, so that you become the vendor of choice.

Summary

Prevent back-outs.
Get commitment.
Deal with the competition.
Ask for referrals and/or introductions.
Show appreciation.
Send personal handwritten notes.
Maintain and develop the relationship for more business.
Be proactive.

C.3 • Prescribing Solutions

Lessons Learned _____

_____

_____

I Commit to Implement:

1. _____

_____

_____

2. _____

_____

_____

3. _____

_____

_____

I Need to Work on:

1. _____

_____

_____

2. _____

_____

_____

The ABC, 123 Sales Results System Reference Summary and Post Call Review

1. **Build Rapport:**

    Find commonality

    Mirror and match physiology, tonality, words

    Open-ended questions—listen

    Determine visual, auditory or kinesthetic

2. **Set Parameters:**

    Time, objective, agenda, end result/outcome, yes/no, permission to ask questions/take notes, interruptions and biggest objection

3. **Buying Motivators:**

    Dig deep, 80/20 rule

    How long has the problem existed?

    What have they done to fix it?

    Why hasn't it worked?

    How much is it costing them or their organization?

    How does it make them feel personally?

4. **Financial Ability:**

    Review three or four problems identified

    "Have you got a budget set aside?"

    No—how do you plan on proceeding?

    Yes— "sharing" and "round numbers"

    Price ranges, bracketing

5. **Decision-making Process:**

    Review of problems and budget

    "When will you be making a decision?"

    "Who 'besides yourself' is involved in the decision-making process?"

6. Summarizing:

Buying motivators, financial ability, decision making

Confirm a yes/no response prior to presentation

In the prospect/client's words and dominant sense

Asking for other issues or problems before proceeding

Know the client's presentation expectations

7. Prescribe Solutions:

Prescriptions—sell today, educate tomorrow

Client's point of view (dominant sense)

Beginning (summary), confirm nothing has changed

Middle (solutions)—features and benefits (draft proposals)

"Which problem would you like me to provide a solution for first?"

Interest Technique: 1 to 10 scale—1 no, 10 yes

Rating under 6—take the fault

Ratings 7-9 —What must I do to get you to a 10?

Let the customer buy—"What would you like me to do next?"

8. Account Retention and Development:

Follow up / buyer's remorse

Show appreciation

Ask for referrals/introductions

Be proactive

Conclusion

You can't build anything without a solid foundation. You learned that A is for Attitude—the foundation of all successful people. The 1,2,3's are attitudes and belief (1) in yourself, (2) in your organization and (3) in your market. Without a positive attitude and belief in all these elements, there is no foundation upon which to build your success.

You have the opportunity to take hold of your attitude, realize it is yours and develop it into a millionaire's attitude. You learned how to overcome fear and deal with rejection, increase productivity and save time and money.

You reflected, confirmed and took hold of your attitude toward your organization, its products and services and fellow team members, while developing an owner's mentality.

You reflected, confirmed and took hold of your attitude toward the market, profiling your ideal prospect while fully understanding your competition. You also created a personal marketing plan to position yourself as the expert in your field.

You could have a fantastic attitude, but a positive attitude alone is not enough to guarantee long-term success. You need goals and an action plan to get you where you want to go. The B is for Behavior—the daily actions that are required to accomplish goals. The 1,2,3's are the goals and behaviors from a (1) personal, (2) organizational and (3) market targeting level. Without these goals and behaviors there is no motivation, no ownership mentality and no drive to go the extra mile.

You learned the relationship between consistent positive behaviors and success. The first step was to learn this on a personal level, for yourself. You identified and developed a personal goal and action plan based on why you come to work.

You followed the same procedures to develop goals, action plans and behaviors for organizational objectives as you did for personal goals, while learning how to improve your time management skills. You became proactive by tracking and monitoring your behaviors.

You learned how to target market your sales efforts through the 80/20 rule and the A,B,C target model while obtaining pertinent industry, organizational and client information. You also created retain, regain and gain strategies.

You then learned about non-traditional sales techniques. The C is for Competency—the capability of following a sales results system with the appropriate competencies to build and maintain long-term relationships. Without this system and without your competencies, time is wasted, and there are no meaningful results. You end up out of control in the buyer's system.

You learned a step-by-step sales results system and the competencies of rapport building to gain trust. In order to build a long-term relationship, you learned that you must first establish rapport. You learned about the relationship selling model, the components of the rapport pie and how to build rapport in the first 30 seconds of meeting someone. You also learned how to identify an individual's predominant sense and how to use that sense to your benefit during the presentation phase.

Once rapport has been established, questions can then be asked. You learned why questions are so important, the type of questions that should be asked and how to deal with questions from the prospect or client without giving free consulting. A series of questioning techniques, and questions, were also reviewed.

When asking questions, you must listen effectively. You assessed your own listening skills, learned the characteristics of good and poor listeners, and learned active listening techniques that you can apply immediately. Always remember these two quotes:

Seek first to understand, if you really want to be understood.

Stephen Covey

Nobody cares how much you know until they know how much you care.

Cavett Robert

You learned how to qualify opportunities by setting the parameters, uncovering buying motivators, financial ability, decision-making processes, and summarizing everything prior to making a proposal or presentation.

Before you can qualify an opportunity, you must first obtain trust by establishing rapport. Without it there will be no answers to your questions. You learned how to set the parameters of a meeting according to a mutually agreed-upon process. This is setting the ground rules, eliminating surprises and having a clear future toward which both parties work.

Once the parameters of the meeting are set, the questions can begin. You learned how to uncover the buying motivators—not just the organizational needs, but the personal emotions of the prospect or client. If there is no pain there is no gain.

You learned how to uncover financial considerations once a number of buying motivators have been identified. This is a critical step in financially qualifying the prospect while providing you with insight into feasible solutions.

Now that you have identified the buying motivators and the financial ability, you must confirm the decision-making process. You learned how to confirm this process and how to deal with committees and other decision makers that you may not be able to get in front of.

Prior to the summary, the buying motivators, financial ability, decision-making process and timing should all have been identified and qualified. This is where you determine whether you have a solution to solve the prospect's problem, within their budget and if you are able to present to the decision makers or not. You learned how to summarize the findings by engaging the prospect or client in a committed way.

Finally, the presentation. You learned how to review the parameters of the presentation, the findings, and how to present prescribed solutions to the prospect's problems, in their dominant sense.

During the presentation stage, you learned how to measure the prospect's reactions and how those reactions lead to the prospect buying the solution, not being sold a solution.

Now that the prospect has purchased the solution, you learned how to maintain the relationship, keep competitors out, develop the account for more business and obtain new prospect introductions and referrals, while remaining in communication on an ongoing basis.

We have discussed attitude, behavior and competencies; however, C also stands for conclusion and commitment. Commitment leads me to the final point I want to make to you relating to the ABC, 123 Sales Results System. Commitment requires discipline. Discipline is a commitment to yourself, to do what you have to do even when you don't want to do it.

It is through self-discipline that you will realize results. However, discipline is hard to master. You will need to discipline yourself for at least 21 consecutive days to make it a habit. To do this you have to identify the appropriate behaviors to reach your goals and monitor yourself daily. Monitoring, or recognizing, yourself gives you the satisfaction of daily accomplishments, or successes, and leads toward increased motivation. This increased motivation is then rewarded in terms of results. Behavior that gets recognized and rewarded gets repeated. Can you discipline yourself for at least 21 days?

You have many charts at your disposal. The best one for you to start using immediately, if you haven't already started to use it, is the Monthly Monitor Chart. Use it to monitor yourself on each skill area in the process that you feel you need to improve on.

Now it is up to you. You have an internationally proven sales results system that you can apply in your daily sales activities. All you have to do now is practice, practice and practice. You have to try it, fall down, get up and do it again and again until you master it. Master these techniques and your selling and communication skills will improve dramatically.

It is not about selling, it is about building relationships and helping people discover their needs and their options. Show your prospects you care and make a memorable selling difference!

The Salesman's Prayer

*Oh creator of all things, help me. For this day I go out into the
world naked and alone, and without your hand to guide me I will
wander far from the path which leads to success and happiness.*

*I ask not for gold or garments or even opportunities equal
to my ability; instead, guide me so that I may acquire
ability equal to my opportunities.*

*You have taught the lion and the eagle how to hunt and prosper
with teeth and claw. Teach me how to hunt with words
and prosper with love so that I may be a lion among
men and an eagle in the marketplace.*

*Help me to remain humble through obstacles and failures; yet hide
not from mine eyes the prize that will come with victory.*

*Assign me tasks in which others have failed; yet guide me
to pluck the seeds of success from their failures. Confront me
with fears that will temper my spirit; yet endow me
with courage to laugh at my misgivings.*

*Spare me sufficient days to reach my goals; yet help
me to live this day as though it be my last.*

*Guide me in my words that they may bear fruit;
yet silence me from gossip that none be maligned.*

*Discipline me in the habit of trying and trying again; yet
show me the way to make use of the law of averages. Favor
me with alertness to recognize opportunity; yet endow me
with patience which will concentrate my strength.*

Bathe me in good habits that the bad ones may drown; yet grant me compassion for weakness in others. Suffer me to know that all things shall pass; yet help me to count my blessings of today.

Expose me to hate so it not be a stranger; yet fill my cup with love to turn strangers into friends.

But all these things be only if they will. I am a small and a lonely grape clutching the vine yet thou hast made me different from all others. Verily, there must be a special place for me. Guide me. Help me. Show me the way.

Let me become all you planned for me when my seed was planted and selected by you to sprout in the vineyard of the world.

Help this humble salesman. Guide me, God.

Og Mandino
The Greatest Salesman in the World
New York: Bantam, 1983

Bibliography

Batchelor, David J. *Skills for Sales Success*. Toronto: Canadian Professional Sales Association, 2000.

Covey, Stephen. *The Seven Habits of Highly Effective People*. New York: Simon and Schuster, 1989.

Domanski, James. *Profiting by Phone—No Nonsense Skills and Techniques for Selling and Getting Leads by Telephone*. Omaha: Business By Phone Inc.

Harvey, Christine. *Secrets of the World's Top Salesperformers*. Arrow Books, 1991.

Girard, Joe. *How to Sell Anything to Anybody*. New York: Warner Books, 1977.

Girard, Joe. *How to Sell Yourself*. New York: Warner Books, 1981.

Gleeson, Kerry. *The Personal Efficiency Program*. New York: John Wiley & Sons, Inc., 1994.

Hill, Napoleon. *The Law of Success*. Chicago: Success Unlimited, Inc., 1979.

Hill, Napoleon. *The Think and Grow Rich Action Pack*. New York: Hawthorn Books Inc., 1972.

Lakin, Alan. *How to Get Control of Your Time and Your Life*. New York: The New American Library, Inc., 1973.

Mandino, Og. *The Greatest Salesman in the World*. New York: Bantam, 1983.

Miller, Robert B. Heiman, Stephen E. *Strategic Selling*. New York: Warner Books, Inc., 1985.

Sandler, David H. *You Can't Teach a Kid to Ride a Bike at a Seminar*. New York: Dutton, 1995.

Urichuck, Bob. *Online for Life: The 12 Disciplines for Living Your Dreams*. Ottawa: Carp, ON: Creative Bound, 2000.

About the Author

Bob Urichuck is a Canadian international professional speaker, trainer and consultant. He is the founding president of the Canadian Association of Professional Speakers (Ottawa), and a past club president of Toastmasters International. Bob has a diploma in adult learning from St. Francis Xavier University. He is a Certified Master Trainer (CMT) and Certified Sales Professional (CSP) who also trains and certifies salespeople through the Canadian Professional Sales Association.

Bob has a proven track record as a successful entrepreneur, motivational speaker, sales trainer, coach and salesman with over 25 years' experience. His experience has taken him from door to door to executive boardroom sales, from product to franchise development, from small business to some of the world's leading corporations, and from small towns in Canada to international destinations like Singapore. He partners with organizations to get bottom-line results in the areas of business development and performance improvement through an ongoing disciplined approach to leadership, motivation, sales and service. He is the author of two books and numerous internationally published articles.

Bob may be contacted directly at bob@bobu.com

Everyone has the potential, and the right,
to live the life of his or her dreams.
Bob Urichuck helps individuals and organizations
identify their objectives and the disciplines
needed to achieve them.
The results are measurable and lasting.

Creative Bound Resources
A division of Creative Bound Inc.
Resources for personal growth and enhanced performance
www.creativebound.com

Supporting the business community
with lifestyle resources for personal growth
and enhanced performance.

Creative Bound authors are experts in a variety of lifestyle areas, including: stress control and life balance, leisure strategies, motivation, mental training (in sports, work and life), goal setting, enhancement of personal and professional performance, healthy relationships—both intimate and professional—and parenting and family management.

Bob Urichuck is recognized as a "2000 Consummate Speaker" (*Sharing Ideas* News Magazine). He speaks internationally on a variety of topics, including motivation, leadership, teamwork, sales and sales management, goal setting, and recognition and praise in a healthy corporation. Keynote presentations are tailored to the needs of each group for optimal impact.

For more information,
please contact
Creative Bound Resources at:
1-800-287-8610
in Ottawa (613) 831-3641
resources@creativebound.com
www.creativebound.com

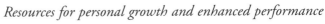
Resources for personal growth and enhanced performance

We hope you have enjoyed
Up Your Bottom Line
Featuring the ABC, 123 Sales Results System

To order additional copies of *Up Your Bottom Line* by Bob Urichuck, please contact Creative Bound Inc. at 1-800-287-8610 (toll-free, North America) or (613) 831-3641. Associations, institutions, businesses and retailers—ask about our wholesale discounts for bulk orders.

ISBN 0-921165-72-2 $21.95 CAN
192 pages $17.95 US

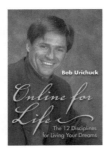

Online for Life:
The 12 Disciplines for Living Your Dreams

Do you know who you are?
Do you love what you're doing?
Do you have what you want out of life?
Do you *know* what you want out of life?
Are you "committed" to anything?
Are you thankful for each new day?

If you answered "no" to any of these questions, but want to say YES! to all of them, this book will inspire you to take control of your life. Bob Urichuck's acclaimed 12 Disciplines will provide you with a step-by-step, *inside-out* approach to finding the authentic you. With discipline, direction, and new tools in hand, you'll soon be living the life of your dreams!

This is an incredible book. It changes lives in very profound ways, and even more important, the changes are not transient, they stick.
—Dr. Sharon Rolbin, author of
Surviving Organizational Insanity

ISBN 0-921165-65-X $19.95 CAN
200 pages $15.95 US

Call to order:
1-800-287-8610
(613) 831-3641 (Ottawa)
Fax: (613) 831-3643

or write to:
Creative Bound Inc.
Box 424, Carp ON
Canada K0A 1L0

info@creativebound.com
www.creativebound.com